CYBER DEFENSE

DOMAIN NAME SYSTEMS
AS THE NEXT PUBLIC UTILITY

HACKERS
ARE SEIZING
THE MOMENT

CYBER DEFENSE

DOMAIN NAME SYSTEMS
AS THE NEXT PUBLIC UTILITY

CRAIG MACKINDER

PUBLISHED IN 2022 BY
KINETICS DESIGN – KDBOOKS.CA

Published in 2022 by
Kinetics Design, KDbooks.ca

ISBN 978-1-988360-73-7 (paperback)
ISBN 978-1-988360-74-4 (ebook)

Cover and interior design, typesetting,
online publishing, and printing by Daniel Crack,
Kinetics Design, KDbooks.ca
www.linkedin.com/in/kdbooks/

Edited by Michael Carroll

Contact the author at
www.craigmackinder.com

Dedicated to my children:
You surely cannot remember a world without today's
Internet. But you may one day recall how we tamed an
unkind, wild, and criminal Internet to make it safe and free
for everyone.

Contents

Foreword

"I saved a life today ..."

It's late afternoon, and as I'm driving home, traffic comes to a crawl. A car has driven over the median strip and slammed into the sidewalk with such force that the front wheels are torn off. The car is now smoking, yet traffic continues to crawl by and no one has stopped to help. As I get closer, I notice there's someone stuck inside. I quickly pull over, run toward the car, and pull the person from the vehicle. Any delays I faced earlier in the day now made sense; I was exactly where I was supposed to be.

Two years after the start of Amazon Web Services, I experienced something similar. I needed help building a scalable platform capable of handling traffic from the likes of Google and Yahoo. Many so-called experts suggested using the cloud, and then I met Craig MacKinder.

Craig's understanding of the core foundation of the Internet led my company to be one of the first to utilize a hybrid approach for our DNS and infrastructure, years ahead of our competitors.

No life was saved, but it was Craig's fundamental understanding of infrastructure that led our company to be accredited by the Media Ratings Council and trusted by the likes of JPMorgan Chase, US Bank, Nestlé, Peapod, Carhartt, Edward Jones, and Fender.

With all the attention on cybersecurity due to hacks, malware attacks, and ransomware, I was surprised to learn that more than half of all corporations have no consolidated view of their physical, virtual, and cloud assets.

On top of that, businesses have been slow to realize how dangerous and threatening DNS-based attacks are. Less than 20 percent of IT professionals are actively monitoring DNS-based exfiltration, and many businesses don't actively monitor changes to their own DNS records. SolarWinds' massive DNS attack in December 2020 was such a disaster, the ramifications of which are still unknown.

From saving a life today to working with Craig MacKinder, sometimes you're exactly where you should be. If you're reading this, you understand that the cracks in the DNS represent a foundational risk of our core Internet capabilities. It appears you, too, are in the right place at the right time.

Jeff Greenfield
SENIOR VICE PRESIDENT
Buy Side — WideOrbit

Introduction

We shouldn't ask our customers to make a tradeoff between privacy and security. We need to offer them the best of both. Ultimately, protecting someone else's data protects all of us.

— TIM COOK, CEO OF APPLE

If 2020 taught us nothing else, it made us realize once again that the unimaginable can become reality faster than we can ever appreciate until it happens. Who would have predicted in February 2020 that the National Football League Super Bowl would be the last time Americans would gather by the tens of thousands to watch a sporting event, that there would be a college basketball March without the madness, that the National Basketball Association and National Hockey League regular seasons would be shut down abruptly, that there would be no Wimbledon tennis or Summer Olympics in Japan?

Late-night talk show hosts and news anchors broadcasted from their living rooms via Skype and Zoom, technologies that saw record profits and became as instrumental in maintaining some level of regular employment in the United States and elsewhere as computers themselves.

As I began writing this book, America was just starting to grapple with a global pandemic the likes of which hadn't been seen in the country in more than a century. Businesses and schools, small and large, were either temporarily or permanently shuttered in the face of statewide stay-at-home orders in nearly all 50 states.

Although the COVID-19 outbreak originated in China in December 2019, by April 2020 it had spread worldwide to over 150 countries. Eventually, tens of millions became infected and millions died due to it. From actor Tom Hanks, to U.K. Prime Minister Boris Johnson, to local grocery clerks, COVID-19 generally didn't discriminate, though poor people and those of color were disproportionately affected by the virus because not everyone was able to work from home.

Most college-educated Americans and those with white-collar jobs were able to continue working and get paid from home in order to avoid being infected, but those in low-wage jobs with no paid leave or health insurance had little choice but to keep going to work. Deep, systemic disparities have been revealed, including the lack of Internet access, the base level of a public good for employment these days.

Nonetheless, many businesses were able to continue operating as usual by enabling their employees to work from home.[1] Millions of Americans who normally did their work within their offices' Internet security infrastructure commenced accessing the Internet from their homes without giving much thought to some of the underlying security challenges of an ad hoc, nation-wide influx of remote workers.

Broad Internet access is the reason so many workers are able to telecommute and not miss a beat, yet one thing this crisis might also reveal is just how vulnerable the Internet is. The danger is due to three words you might have heard of but don't understand — the Domain Name System, or DNS.

Since most of us have no idea what happens in the background when we type a web address into a uniform resource locator (URL), the average person might ask, "Why should I care as long as I get to my website?" Here are three reasons everyone should care:

- When you type in a web address or begin a search online, there are several operations that happen in milliseconds before your website appears. In that short bit of time, as your computer attempts to locate the web address you're seeking, that communiqué can be intercepted and exfiltrated by a third or fourth party hacking into your system.

- The question the average person has never asked, and most haven't even thought to care about, is who actually controls the Internet? Actually, there are about a dozen organizations around the world that control the Internet. Every website, every person who has ever gotten online, anything and everything ever done on the web, is stored on servers somewhere and only those organizations have a bird's-eye view of it all.

- Regardless of how strong any entity's security infrastructure might be, the Internet, at its core, lacks any kind of security infrastructure. No system is safe from that kind of vulnerability as long as it operates in cyberspace.

In this book, my argument is twofold. First, we no longer have the luxury of debating the inherent vulnerabilities associated with our modern DNS. This crisis has made it urgent that we do something about it now. And second, the Internet has become so essential and so commoditized that it should be treated as a utility, including making the DNS more localized and controlled by American entities. I'll argue that our local, county, and state governments rather than some mysterious third or fourth party should monitor server traffic locally instead of through remote servers where the opportunities for hacking and what's called *DNSpionage* are greatest.[2]

To date, large-scale hacks of businesses and government entities have shocked the system and caused individual web owners and network administrators to add layers and layers of encryption and firewalls to prevent future hacks. All of those layers do nothing to deal with the fundamental insecurity at the heart of the Internet. With the right information, bad actors could do irreparable damage to the Internet and conduct espionage and hackings on a scale never seen before.

One consequence of all that has happened in the face of the COVID-19 pandemic is the way that people work in America has changed, perhaps for good. Many Americans, in fact, close to 60 percent, were already working from home at least part of the time before the pandemic, but full-time remote workers made up less than 10 percent of the workforce. Now the reverse is true.

With so many new remote workers taxing servers and security infrastructures, it's time to confront the problem that prior to the COVID-19 pandemic has only vexed information technology (IT) professionals for years — how do we fix the spine, the core, the backbone of the Internet, the Domain Name System, without disrupting the Internet before a catastrophic hack of the DNS kills the World Wide Web (WWW)?

PART ONE

HOW WE GOT HERE

DEFENSE

INTERNET
SECURITY
TAKES A BACK
SEAT IN THE
PANDEMIC

1

Pandemic Proves
"Internet Is Essential"

A novel and lethal virus for which there is no human immunity, a vaccine at least a year and a half away, and the only way to stop it from continuing to spread to millions of people around the globe and killing millions is for all of us to physically distance ourselves from one another. In a nutshell, that's how we got here.

Here is where suddenly physical distancing is the norm as is remote work. Sounds more like the plot of a Hollywood science fiction flick, but it is, in fact, our collective new reality. While this global disruption to a world order that has been fairly stable for the past several decades has caused us to contemplate the many societal changes COVID-19 has wrought, it's fair to say that in a crisis not much thought has been given to the rushed nature of our transition to the new ways social distancing has changed the way we work and interact online.

For several years prior to the COVID-19 outbreak hitting the United States, remote work had been on the rise. The more ubiquitous wireless technology has become, the more options businesses and workers have had to work remotely. Just two years ago, nearly 30 percent of Americans worked from home [1]

But clearly the pandemic has been the impetus for the dramatic increase from part of the workforce experimenting with work-from-home options to remote work becoming standard.[2] What that means for security and access is deep and complex and we have little time to wrap our heads around it.

The coronavirus pandemic onslaught in early March 2020 brought an acute awareness to many people that the Internet is essential. While this is a truism today, there are still millions of Americans who don't have access to the Internet. In turn, those numbers reveal the woeful disparity in socio-economics for people based on whether they have higher education with white-collar jobs or are low-wage earners with only a high school education.[3]

A dark side to the essentiality of the Internet and the lack of public options for broader access is being revealed. Not everyone has access to the Internet, even though they also need essential services that are more and more becoming available only online. For example, television footage of thousands of people lining up for unemployment forms in Florida was just one example of U.S. citizens putting themselves at risk of catching a pandemic virus because they either didn't have Internet access or the website for unemployment was mostly unusable — a strong argument for why the Internet should be a public utility available to all.

The choice between whether you can afford to socially distance yourself versus risking infection to put food on the table when remote work isn't an option seems very Darwinian for the leading democracy in the world. Yet if you happen to have a college degree and are on the higher end of the pay scale, you're more likely to ride out the outbreak working from home without losing job or pay.

The U.S. Bureau of Labor Statistics reported that nearly half of those with college degrees aged 25 years old or more worked from home before the pandemic. On the other hand, only about 3.2 percent of workers with less than a high school diploma had the luxury to do so.[4] Those jobs are made up of waiters and waitresses, bus drivers, delivery drivers, and service jobs in general where the livelihood depends on customers going out to dinner, the movies, the theater, or work, et cetera.

And let's not forget the first responders and medical workers on the front line of the COVID-19 outbreak who got sick while helping others suffering from the disease. No matter how crucial the Internet is, there are still some things that require human-to-human contact, but for everything else, frankly, the Internet is essential. Still, now rather than later is the time to make sure we don't create the breeding ground for an Internet pandemic while we're at it.

Internet Security Takes a Back Seat … Again

In March 2020, as the number of infections in the United States climbed, the U.S. Congress passed a bill to deal with the outbreak and pay people directly so that everyone from state to state no matter their income level could stay home to "flatten the curve" of the pandemic. Stay-at-home orders lasted months well into the summer with the threat that even if the virus was isolated and defeated, it could resurge as it did in Japan. That meant that professionals, especially in high-paying, white-collar jobs would continue to fill the air with data flowing over wireless networks to create a virtual gold mine for hackers.

At the same time that many businesses were fortunate for the option to transition their employees rapidly to remote work, for IT professionals, the fear that not all businesses and universities were prepared for the security challenges involved in remote work has steadily grown. As the saying goes, "only fools rush in," but the outbreak left businesses and universities little choice but to scale back rapidly from office-based to remote work. Without much consideration given to the rushed nature of generating millions of new remote workers, some in very high-security white-collar jobs, servers around the world have become treasure troves of data for hackers seeking high-value data in some of the most frequently targeted industries.

Major employers such as Blue Cross Blue Shield allowed thousands of employees to work from home. More than an eighth of the 35,000 employees of the health insurance provider began working from home in one week.[5] In March 2020 on the West Coast, Cox Communication, a major cable provider, sent all its employees capable of working from home to do so. State Farm, United Health Care, large financial institutions, and big universities all shut down their offices and grounded their traveling employees. How secure is the data being accessed from home now? Even traveling professionals can be lax in prioritizing Internet security while on the road or working from home, but new employees didn't have the time to be briefed and brought up to speed.

That's simply considering the typical Internet security protocols like securing networks with multi-authentication and virtual private networks (VPNs). What about the totally unencrypted DNS upon which all security protocols are built? The Internet is still vulnerable to the fundamental security breach at the core of the web. At a moment when we don't have the luxury of time, time is of the essence in solving the DNS problem before it's too late.

Top Universities' Dangerous Scramble to Provide Online Classes

By and large, hackers targeting the United States are looking for data. One of the best places to find it is in America's top universities. Some of the best colleges and universities in the world are in the United States, and at the beginning of March 2020, one by one, they started to close their campuses.[6] First, it was the likes of Harvard and Ohio State that shut down, and then the Big Ten college conference as a whole followed suit, but it wasn't as simple as canceling classes for the year as many primary and secondary schools did. Students at these schools were in the middle of earning degrees; many were set to graduate in just two months.

Instead, these universities, in the same way businesses quickly transitioned their staff to remote work, had to quickly become online institutions and have their professors turn their lectures into webinars. Dorms were emptied as students were sent home to finish their semesters. That left potentially hundreds of thousands of students without the proper Internet access in their hometowns with little options for finishing school.

On top of that conundrum, there was also the risk posed by millions of young adults and teenagers remotely learning on new online tools that they might not have been savvy enough to use safely. Stanford University, one of the creators of the Internet, has its own application data standards and a whole website devoted to guiding remote students and staff on telecommuting, but not every school was so prepared.

All organizations had to create their own risk assessments and data classifications, but it's sometimes hard to tell where risk assessment ends and data classification begins. That's why developing a policy helps to communicate the risk and provide a classification system for how to handle different data types based on risk severity. Understanding those risks from a DNS management perspective was largely missing but incredibly critical.

However, securing the DNS system has to involve a risk assessment for both data and application dangers. In fact, data-security specialists commence typical penetration tests by analyzing attack vectors where the DNS systems and services can be exploited. Specifically, when analyzing outward-facing systems, say, public operating ones like a public computer or a business's Wi-Fi, a security researcher, by analyzing DNS, can find the names and Internet protocol (IP) address locations of publicly available systems.

The result is the discovery of many new ways to attack the system at different system entry points, or as IT experts call it, attack vectors. But because there was little time to consider all options and ramifications at the onset of the pandemic, universities initiated testing online teaching on the fly with little preparation for all security gaps.

Zoom's Profits Soar as Schools and Universities Close

Former New York City Mayor Bill de Blasio announced in April 2020 that the metropolis was canceling all public schooling for the rest of the year. State and local governments had to guess way ahead of time where they would be several months later in order to prepare for a long wait to get back to normal, if ever. Two tech companies in particular have benefited from this new normal: Zoom and Cisco saw, and continue to enjoy, record profits as business entities, major universities, entertainers, and public officials turned to their video-conferencing software to manage virtual face-to-face interactions such as online classes and business conferences.[7]

So far there has been no major security breach that we know of involving online education or a video-conferencing provider. But it's like the joke told by Steve McQueen's character to Yul Brynner's in John Sturges's 1960 movie *The Magnificent Seven*:

Vin: *Reminds me of that fellow back home that fell off a ten-story building.*

Chris: *What about him?*

Vin: *Well, as he was falling, people on each floor kept hearing him say, "So far, so good."*

Well, let's just say so far so good when it comes to our new normal for online work and education. However, just as a pandemic of this scale was predictable, so are the dangers posed by a globally connected Internet that has become so integral to how the world functions that it's deemed essential but yet is insecure at its core.

Many Changes in Telecommunications Will Be Permanent

Without question, many of the changes to the way we live and work will last long into the foreseeable future and some will be permanent. Businesses large and small are realizing savings in overhead and office space by allowing greater numbers of employees to work from home out of necessity. If we manage to get the pandemic under control, those savings are going to determine whether or not those changes are permanent.

Yet work and school are only two pillars of society undergoing lasting transformations and relying much more heavily on telecommunications over person-to-person interaction. There are many facets of everyday life where telecommunications on the Internet before the pandemic arrived were legally barred but are now becoming the norm. Let's take changes in medicine and health care first where Health Insurance Portability and Accountability Act

(HIPPA) laws protecting private information prevented doctors and hospitals from utilizing telemedicine on a large scale.

Two areas where medical professionals predict permanent changes to the way medicine is delivered concern Medicare and telecommunication tools. Up until now, medical billing for Medicaid and Medicare patients for tele-medical visits couldn't be done because telemedicine over Facetime or Skype wasn't allowed.[8] Those rules have been relaxed to permit people isolated at home to communicate with their doctors over the Internet. It's also helping people who aren't affected by COVID-19 to still make doctors' appointments without risking their health by going to the office or hospital.

The U.S. government and the way Congress function changed during the COVID-19 pandemic, too. COVID-19 made it necessary for gatherings of large groups to be conducted remotely, including those of hundreds of congresspeople and senators who would have normally met in the Capitol to enact legislation. Instead, hearings and sessions were done via video confer-encing, with just a few essential persons on the floor inside Congress. A plus for constituents was that many members of Congress who were out of touch with their districts could now live full-time there and be closer to the people they represented as opposed to spending much of their time in Washington, D.C.

In the midst of the pandemic, 2020 being an election year put added pressure on states and governors to manage local elections while keeping the population safe. One answer was to allow mail-in balloting, but that also added ammunition against the idea of voting electronically. At the very beginning of the pandemic in the United States, there were several primaries administered atrociously, resulting in a spike in COVID-19 infections when voters were forced to vote in person.

Some states where mail-in balloting was allowed enabled voters to avoid long lines and infection spikes, but counting the votes took days and in some cases nearly a week. Important to our discussion here is the security of such a system where people are able to vote online or via their mobile devices. Russia infiltrated the 2016 election and has never stopped. Shifting to electronic balloting before the system is prepared to secure those votes is risky. However, most Americans might not realize that electronic and mobile voting has been used for a decade by our military and the disabled.

We know it can be done and that it could help make voting safer and easier, thereby increasing participation. Yet we shouldn't take lightly the risks involved with electronic voting going from a small portion of our society to the standard way for people to vote, especially when so much data online is being targeted by bad actors meant to do harm in light of the influx of remote work and data online that otherwise would be harder to get. Imagine what Russia would do to disrupt an election where all votes were cast and tabulated over the Internet.

Hackers Are Seizing the Moment

If a pandemic resulting in depression-level economic numbers wasn't enough, hackers are taking advantage of the new work-from-home model sweeping the globe almost exclusively in the United States. In fact, a Russian-backed group of hackers with ties to the Russian spy arm, the Federal Security Service (Russian acronym FSB, formerly the KGB), have already started testing their capabilities and increasing their powers since the beginning of 2020.

This new method of attack is unique in the way it manages to infect systems. Instead of trying to hack through individual corporate firewalls, hackers try to exploit employees accessing their corporate systems. First, they identify remote workers logging into their company's virtual private network meant to secure access to the network. Once users go to another less secure website, the hackers wait until they log into their VPNs. At that point, the hackers are able to unleash ransomware into a corporate system.

A warning for how dangerous this new method of attack can be was summed up by the technical director for Symantec, a top Internet security company that monitors corporate and government hacks: "Right now this is all about making money, but the infrastructure they are deploying could be used to wipe out a lot of data — and not just at corporations."[9]

Evil Corp, as the Russian-sponsored hackers call themselves, has been testing major U.S. corporations' networks in novel ways to pull off bigger and more devastating attacks. Using the most advanced ransomware, already they've attacked entire cities in the United States, including Baltimore, Maryland, and Atlanta, Georgia.[10] They even infiltrated city electoral systems in Louisiana in advance of its May 2020 primaries.

The Federal Bureau of Investigation (FBI), along with the Department of Homeland Security (DHS), issued alerts warning elected officials as well as large corporations in the United States about the potential dangers not only to corporations but also to the entire election system in America. Businesses have had their systems frozen through ransomware, but the difference is, instead of asking for thousands or even hundreds of thousands of dollars, these thieves expect to make really big financial scores and threaten to delete data unless corporations hand over up to $50 million in some instances.

When it comes to election infrastructure, there's no limit to the chaos that could be caused if election systems were frozen, ballots were stolen, or voter roll data was manipulated. Attempts have been made at every level from the federal government all the way to local clerks of courts. The fact that some of these attacks aren't the typical ransomware hacks where data is eventually released once the blackmail is paid is even more alarming. This new group is looking to completely wipe out data, a bad sign for any assault on elections.

Despite the fact that it's been well known and established by all intelligence agencies in the United States that Russia infiltrated and affected the 2016 presidential election, sanctions and indictments have done little to deter them. Moreover, little has been done to pass legislation that would strengthen and secure America's election system. And Russian hackers aren't alone in exploiting these vulnerabilities.

While Russia is clearly the main adversary attempting to disrupt and distort America's electoral and political systems, it's not the only nation-state hacker getting in on the sudden wealth of cyber data floating in the ether. China has also sponsored hackers aiming to infiltrate American universities and research facilities, particularly those working on new COVID-19 vaccines.[11]

Two Kids from Two Different Worlds

Arguing for more local government control of servers and networks in the United States, as I am in this book, isn't limited to security risks. As a public good, the Internet's essentiality in this moment is leaving many Americans behind because it hasn't been treated as critical as electricity, water, or gas. That's left millions of households in dire straits. Without access to the Internet, all of these permanent changes to the way we live and work will leave millions of Americans limited in their job opportunities, their access to health care, and their right to a quality education.

Imagine the lives of two different kids living in America. One lives in Valdosta, Georgia, a city with the lowest Internet access in America. Only 55 percent of households there have the Internet and a full 22 percent don't even own a computer.[12] Compare that to a kid growing up in Washington State where nearly 90 percent of households have access to the Internet.[13]

These disparities are reflected in the demographics, as well. In the same way that COVID-19 hit poor, rural, and minority communities the hardest, those same underlying inequities reflect those in the United States who, without making the Internet a public utility, will undoubtedly suffer the most from this new way of working and living.

When primary and secondary schools across the United States closed for the year, many students were able to continue learning on tablets or home computers. However, many weren't. According to an Associated Press 2019 analysis, the percent of households without a home computer or Internet access in the United States is 17 and 18 respectively.[14] Southern students are going to suffer the most, since Southern states make up the majority of those with the least amount of Internet access among their populations.

For both these reasons — security and equity — it's imperative that local governments urgently work toward making Internet access a public utility available to all citizens in light of the new world the pandemic has created. On top of that, security can't take a back seat this time. If we're to depend on local servers to provide access, we have to ensure the Internet is more secure than it is right now. So how do we make these fixes? It begins with understanding how the Internet works and that starts with understanding how it came to be what it is today.

2

The Orgs That Created
(and Control) the Internet

In 2014, the United States did something extraordinarily controversial that barely made a whimper in the country. IT professionals knew
about it, and some Republicans made a fuss, but it largely went unnoticed. In
essence, the United States gave up ultimate control of the Internet to a global
body consisting of people and organizations from countries around the world.

Ironically, the Internet initially was a top-secret U.S. military program that
sought to devise a way to communicate on the battlefield without using radio
waves that could be intercepted by enemies. The U.S. military initiated this by
thinking, *What if we could send a message in code that could be translated into
words on the other end on a closed network that can't be intercepted?*

That work commenced in the early 1960s. Over two decades, slowly but
surely, the U.S. government built the foundation of a new technology that just
40 years later was deemed essential worldwide.

Who Built the Internet (and Why)?

At what has been called the "Mother of All Demos,"[1] Doug Engelbart, an engi-
neer and inventor at the Stanford Research Institute (SRI), unveiled a number
of firsts: the mouse, video-conferencing capabilities, a demonstration of a
computer as a word processor that could display graphics, and hyperlinks.
Engelbart's presentation of these new computer advances didn't happen in the
1980s or 1990s; it occurred in 1968!

Despite the "wow factor" in this revelation, the ability for systems to
communicate was still far off. Connecting a couple of computers on the
same network proved to be the *easy* part. The biggest challenge was to get
one network of computers to communicate with another. There had to
be a common language, a mutual architecture, that would let two different
networks send and receive data.

By 1969, the first Internet was born. Developed in an effort to bridge that communication divide, the U.S. Defense Advanced Research Projects Agency (DARPA) created the Advanced Research Projects Agency Network (ARPANET), the computer network that's considered the first Internet. Within the same year, the first message was sent over the "Internet" from a student at the University of California at Los Angeles (UCLA) to the SRI. For the first time, two computers "talked" with each other despite being hundreds of miles apart.

Although the transmission only sent part of the message, it was still a historic achievement and set up the foundation of the modern Internet as we know it. Just the letters *l-o* of the word *login* made it to the SRI and then the server crashed. But it was a promising start that researchers from around the world continued to build upon.

Keep in mind that this was all in an effort to develop communication capabilities for the U.S. military and intelligence agencies. Sending messages merely a couple of hundred miles and then crashing wouldn't cut it. DARPA researchers were trying to figure out a way to send messages thousands of miles to more than 70 different nations around the globe, not to mention the hundreds of military bases that would have to be connected to the ARPANET.

Four years after that first semi-successful transmission from UCLA to SRI, DARPA researchers sent the first inter-network message in 1973. Computers in London and Norway were the first to connect to the ARPANET, making this the first "global computer network."[2] *Inter-network* became *Internet*, and that's how the first Internet was born.

After the success of the global transmission, DARPA worked quickly to expand the network's reach, connecting the ARPANET to computers at government agencies and universities across the globe. The next year, two researchers from DARPA, Robert Kahn and Vint Cerf, came up with a universal language and rules to govern the way computer networks communicated with one another.

This was no small accomplishment. Essentially, Kahn and Cerf had to devise a rigid set of criteria for transferring data while also allowing for different types of data to be sent and received. In other words, the rules had to be strict but flexible. Thankfully, the two men did just that, inventing what we now know as the transmission control protocol (TCP). The protocol enabled different networks to speak to each other by creating a "gateway" as a means to connect one to the other as opposed to individual files attempting to communicate with a separate network. It also made it so that one network didn't have to have a particular structure to receive data. But there were two points in the TCP that were game changers, setting the stage for the modern Internet.

First, in designing the TCP, Cerf and Kahn built it so that it could grow and expand freely. That meant that there could be no centralized control over the distribution of data. These two researchers were way ahead of their time, because building the TCP with the ability to scale up and grow without centralized control or the need for each network to make internal changes to connect is the basis and foundation of something these two couldn't have fathomed in 1973 — the World Wide Web.

TCP Created the First ISP

Cerf and Kahn's conception of the TCP opened the door to commercial use of this new technology. Researchers unveiled the TCP in 1974, and soon after, ARPANET was commercialized as Telenet, the first Internet service provider (ISP) in history. Considering how enormously profitable that last step would become, it's amazing to think that Cerf and Kahn didn't even attempt to patent or restrict the use of their designs. If they had, there might have never been a World Wide Web. In the interest of progress, they made their discoveries available to the world.

The missing link in the chain, the IP, was sandwiched between the TCP on the sender's end and the TCP on the receiver's end, and to this day, that's how we send and receive information on the Internet. The TCP sends a package of data while the IP moves the package via router from the sender's IP address to the end user's IP address where the TCP reassembles the data package for viewing, illustrated as shown in Fig. 1.

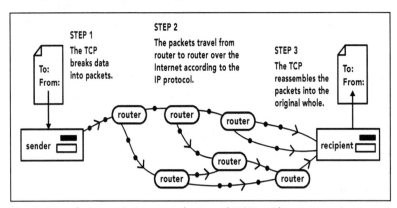

Fig. 1 How the transmission control protocol (TCP) works.
Source: www.zmescience.com/science/who-invented-the-internet-05264.

From that point, evolutionary changes happened annually. Just a year after the TCP was created, there were at least 60 "nodes" connected to the ARPANET. In 1977, the first modem was invented, blazing a new path for home-based computers to connect to the Internet. The first Internet message board appeared in 1979 on Usenet.

The TCP/IP protocol was made the standard for the ARPANET in 1982. By 1986, the Internet officially left military control and was handed over to the National Science Foundation.[3] In fact, it had long since ceased being primarily a military tool and was mostly used in academia to share files and send messages. Moreover, it would be universities and tech pioneers who took the Internet to the next level to conceive the worldwide phenomenon so essential to everyday life in the 21st century.

Researchers and Institutes That Created (and Control) the Internet

If any of the early developers of the modern Internet had at any point limited access based on ownership through patents or private corporations, we wouldn't be discussing the Internet now. It's reasonable to assume that no entity on its own could have created the vast mosaic that is the modern Internet. Consider this: the University of Illinois was responsible for creating the first browser. It used money granted from the National Science Foundation to do so. However, the technology behind building the initial browser was developed in Switzerland. Netscape commercialized it and Microsoft secured the licensing that made it available to everyone.

That type of non-centralized control has been the ethos at the core of the Internet. As mentioned before, Cerf and Kahn could have potentially broken records on human wealth if they'd kept their game-changing innovation to themselves. Instead, in 1992, the pair helped to form the Internet Society whose mission is "to promote the open development, evolution, and use of the Internet for the benefit of all people throughout the world."[4]

While no single entity actually controls the Internet, it's governed by multinational stakeholders. The Internet Architecture Board (IAB), for instance, was part of DARPA and is charged with oversight of the architecture of the Internet. The Internet Assigned Numbers Authority (IANA) is charged with oversight of how IP addresses are allocated, manages a portion of the DNS, and among other things, functions within the Internet Corporation for Assigned Names and Numbers (ICANN). ICANN, along with the functions of IANA, were both under contract with the U.S. Department of Commerce until 2016.

I'll dig further into the importance of ICANN and IANA to the DNS later in this chapter. But for now, those are a few of the organizations in charge of maintaining the standard protocols and maintenance of the "root zones" of the Internet — basically, the nuts and bolts and underpinnings of the Internet, such as how IP addresses are assigned, how websites are registered and maintained, and everything else that enables the Internet to function.

Other organizations, largely nonprofit, were either initially formed under DARPA or are parts of the Internet Society co-founded by Cerf and Kahn, including the Internet Engineering Steering Group, the North American Network Operators' Group, the World Wide Web Consortium, and the Internet Research Task Force, among others. These groups are part of what's referred to as "multinational stakeholders."

Those stakeholders also include research organizations around the world. There's the Asia Pacific Network Information Centre (APNIC), the African Network Information Centre, and the University Corporation for Advanced Internet Development, as well as the Réseaux IP Européens (RIPE) Network Coordination Centre and the Latin America and Caribbean Network Information Centre (LACNIC).

International Internet Governors

There are also stakeholders that look at Internet governance holistically as a global resource. These forums provide space for international discussions from all stakeholders on Internet governance and make recommendations based on those discussions. Some of the most influential of the international Internet governors include the Internet Governance Forum (IGF) established by the United Nations in 2006. This group invites participation from all stakeholders from academia, to corporations, to governments to discuss policy regarding Internet governance.[5]

The World Summit on the Information Society (WSIS) was another body formed by the United Nations in 2003. Its goal is to bridge the gap in Internet access between poor and rich countries. It held summits in 2003 and 2005. The Working Group on Internet Governance came to be as a result of those summits as a means for the United Nations to continue working on bridging the gap.

Dot-Coms and Corporate Internet Control

There are also corporate stakeholders involved in global Internet governance. Some of the biggest and most well-known tech companies are among the dot-coms and corporations with their hands in the pot. Those entities include, among others:

- Amazon.
- AOL.
- eBay.
- Facebook.
- Google.
- Instagram.
- LinkedIn.
- Twitter.
- YouTube.

In essence, since the autumn of 2016, the United States ceased being the ultimate arbiter of Internet governance and ceded control to all of these stakeholders. This, as I said at the beginning, seemed to be controversial, even extraordinary. But as Internet security concerns from all nations, including those about the U.S. government, began to grow, it was necessary for the United States to allow more neutral and global oversight. Considering the breadth and depth of the stakeholders, the United States only ensured the continued freedom of the Internet by relinquishing control.

Who Controls the DNS?

Ironically, the controversy over the decision of the United States to surrender control was superficial. True, the Internet at its roots started as a U.S. military technology, and before the official handover of control took place, the National Telecommunications and Information Administration (NTIA) under the U.S. Department of Commerce had ultimate command over the Internet. ICANN was responsible for managing IANA through the Department of Commerce, but any recommendations made by the organization could be overruled by the U.S. Department of Commerce.[6] That's what changed.

Still, Republicans in the U.S. Congress tried to put a stop to this transition that had been in the works for nearly 20 years at the time. Senator Ted Cruz of Texas, one of the most vocal, claimed the move would be a "giveaway of our Internet freedom." In response, corporate stakeholders such as Google, Twitter, Amazon, and Facebook urged Congress not to stand in the way of this change with a letter that in part said: "A global, interoperable and stable Internet is essential for our economic and national security, and we remain committed to completing the nearly twenty-year transition to the multi-stakeholder model that will best serve U.S. interests."[7]

A more important question than who controls the Internet — obviously no one, really — is who controls the DNS. And that responsibility has been given to ICANN. Based in California, ICANN was initially formed by the Department of Commerce in the late 1990s. Since then, the multi-stakeholder group has been operating under a government contract secured from the U.S. Department of Commerce. It was charged with managing the Internet but with the goal of eventually renouncing ultimate control.

Despite the small dust-up from Republican lawmakers, the transition did, in fact, happen. After it was made official, the chairman of the board of ICANN released a statement applauding the work of the many different global governments, corporations, and individuals that made the change possible, adding, "a governance model defined by the inclusion of all voices, including business, academics, technical experts, civil society, governments and many others is the best way to assure that the internet of tomorrow remains as free, open, and accessible as the internet of today."[8]

What does it mean that ICANN now controls the DNS, the literal spine of the Internet? It's the backbone that holds it up and holds it together, it's how those early messages went back and forth with the letters *l-o* and became *login* on the other end, and it's why we type words into search engines instead of IP addresses. And as this point will illustrate, it's why the Internet as a whole is so vulnerable — not because ICANN controls it but because the DNS itself is completely unencrypted.

For the purposes of the discussion in this chapter, I'll give a quick overview of what the DNS is. In a nutshell, when you type in a web address into your URL, it's the DNS that recognizes the data you input and is able to direct whichever server contains that data to display it on your computer. You see words and letters, but the DNS recognizes numbers and is able to translate and retrieve what you're looking for in split seconds. All of that information — the governing protocols, algorithms, and operations — is stored in one place and managed by a single entity: IANA. Which, as stated earlier, is and always has been overseen by ICANN, the manager of the naming system — how websites are registered and named.

Unlike the societal debate over what handing over the Internet to a collective international body means for freedom of speech, control of DNS in tech circles and soon in government circles revolves around securing the fundamental structure of the Internet's naming system. In reality, the social and societal aspects of the Internet have always had many eyeballs overseeing and regulating how it operates. The truth is that management of ICANN is global with more than 110 countries included in the organization's Government Advisory Committee, most of them members of the United Nations.

Another California-based entity is also in charge of managing a big chunk and frankly the most dangerous chunk of the DNS. Packet Clearing House (PCH) is a nonprofit charged with oversight of some of the most at-risk domains in the DNS.[9] These are sites that are most vulnerable to DNSpionage. In total, there are more than 500 top level domains (TLDs), many based in the Middle East, that are monitored and managed by PCH. It's in that area of concern that this book argues for more localized DNS that can secure the backbone of the Internet from DNSpionage.

Stanford Research Institute and UC Berkeley Helped Create Unencrypted DNS

When you think about how the Internet came to be, mostly through academia and businesses experimenting with this new technology, it's easy to see why and how securing the DNS took a back seat. In the beginning, it was more about making sure the Internet could make a connection. Few really anticipated the type of bad actors and malicious hackers that soon found opportunities in this new global connectivity.

Before there was an official DNS, at the earliest stages, the Stanford Research Institute maintained a simple host file. All of the names and addresses of the original members of the ARPANET network were maintained by the HOSTS. TXT file managed by SRI. At the same time, the University of California at Berkeley had developed its own DNS management system called UNIX. The group at Berkeley was experimenting with how to connect networks when it devised its UNIX system, but as their network grew, it was necessary to create a way to manage all of their member host names and addresses and thus the Berkeley Internet Name Domain (BIND) server was created.

Because Berkeley's DNS had grown so large, it became the standard for sending email exchanges on its campus. By 1985, it was so huge that it became a big part of DARPA's email exchange. From that point on, researchers at Berkeley took the lead on developing the DNS. The mission from the researchers' point of view was to find a uniform way for networks around the world to connect to the Internet. There was little discussion back then about securing the DNS through encryption. It's not really a shortcoming; no one really could have envisioned what the Internet would become today with its ubiquity and the dangers that entails.

However, the risks are well known now and the vulnerabilities are evident to most IT professionals. Since the 1980s when the first DNS system connected several dozen networks, the explosion of the Internet makes the global DNS that much more imperiled. ICANN, in tandem with IANA, largely focuses on DNS work that includes introducing and monitoring TLDs, managing the root nameservers, assigning IP addresses, and maintaining Internet registries around the world. As this discussion moves forward, clearly these entities are going to have to play a large part in securing the DNS, but I'll show that localizing DNS is the best way forward.

CYBERDEFENSE

3

The ARPANET's Achilles' Heel

Remember when almost all website addresses ended in *.net*? It's a throwback to the first Internet — the ARPANET. We say that was the first Internet, but really it is its predecessor. It didn't work quite like the modern one, but everything we know as the World Wide Web today is built upon the early structure of the ARPANET. To understand our current dilemma with the DNS, you have to comprehend the architecture the entire Internet rests on.

In its earliest phase, the Internet began with closed networks called nodes. The network might consist of a group of several researchers working on the same system in the same building, initially in the same room as one another. Testing the ability for one computer to talk to the other required a way for each within the network node to recognize the other. If you worked in an office that used computers in the early to late 1980s, your work computer was used largely to send and share text files within your physical office building.

You didn't communicate with computers outside your network. At first, computers in an office setting were more like virtual files. You could store documents in different folders and your network administrator backed up all the information on your office server. But what if you could send that information to a different location where you shared a network, say, your company's head office in another city, state, or province? The remote system would have to recognize the data coming from your office network's physical location.

Every network node would have to use the same name for one computer to read a shared file from the host or the originator of the document. There was no system to record or map names to match them on a shared network. There had to be a uniform way for one file originated in one system to be shared and read in another. The solution was the HOSTS.TXT protocol. You saved your file in a text file that could be shared and opened by another computer on your network.

However, as networks grew, sharing expanded, and the overloaded HOSTS.TXT naming system couldn't sustain what was fast becoming the modern Internet. There had to be a way to decentralize the naming system so that individual users could create their own host files, their own websites, and networks outside of centralized control could talk to one another. That's when the originators of the Internet came up with the DNS.

Computers communicate using numbers, but humans don't work that way. It's hard enough to remember a seven-digit phone number. Imagine having to know the IP address —10 to 16 digits — for every website you wanted to visit. There would be no Internet as we know it if that had been the case. A simpler way had to be devised for users to access Internet content without memorizing IP addresses. The solution? Memorize "words" like *google.com*.

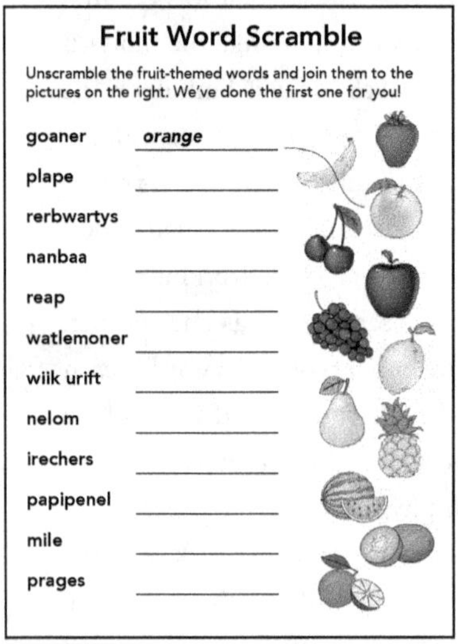

Fig. 2   Fruit Word Scramble.
Source: Courtesy of www.activityvillage. co.uk/fruit-word-scramble. Copyright © 2020 Activity Village. All rights reserved.

When you type in that address, your computer instantaneously reinterprets it into numbers and begins to send out the address in the numerical form you typed in words, as represented in Fig. 2.

You type in the word *orange* and your computer checks the domain name *orange* except it's in computer jargon (*goaner*) and returns to your screen the picture of the *orange* you requested. As in the word scramble in Fig. 2, it might have to wriggle around some other addresses before reaching your query, though, and that's where bad actors can jump in.

Notice something odd about the thing that fundamentally makes the Internet accessible to every user? Notice how your query doesn't go through any kind of encryption to match *goaner* to the picture of an orange? And therein lies the Achilles' heel of the Internet. The DNS is completely unencrypted! It's literally as simple as that, leaving the Internet's foundation wide open to DNSpionage and hacks that could bring the whole thing down.

DNS Rapidly Changed the Internet from Network Control to User Control

To understand the scale of the problem, consider that the word scramble in Fig. 2 represents one user accessing the Internet one time to find the image of an orange. That same user will access multiple websites and search queries throughout the day, each time, behind the scenes, his or her desktop computer, laptop, or smartphone will perform this same operation. Now multiply that by the billions of users around the world accessing the Internet. Each one of these word scramble searches is unencrypted and vulnerable to a massive Internet-wide hack.

You might wonder, why didn't the early designers of the Internet account for this gaping hole in its security? The simple answer is that no one had anticipated most of the security challenges from hackers. In fact, the first virus to be discovered on the Internet didn't happen until 1999, and it wasn't attacking the DNS but rather exploiting vulnerabilities in users' personal computers, namely, by sneaking into their address books.

As ARPANET went from closed networks connecting one node to another to individual users linking to a single big network, the Internet grew bigger and bigger. This is the way computer scientists Paul V. Mockapetris and Kevin J. Dunlap put it:

> ARPANET's role had changed from being a single network connecting large timesharing systems to being one of the several long-haul backbone networks linking local networks which were in turn populated with workstations. The number of hosts changed from the number of timesharing systems (roughly organizations) to the number of workstations (roughly users).[1]

As previously mentioned, the first Internet virus happened a full 15 years after the DNS was first implemented in 1984. That publication changed everything for users. It made personal computers possible and was able to simplify Internet access in a way that made typing the word *orange* take less time and the operations looking for it could resolve themselves easily through the DNS host files. However, some users and networks at the time tried to stick to the old HOSTS.TXT file protocol that originally translated words into IP addresses, since it kept the control in the user or network administrator's hand.

Yet as the majority of websites started operating under the newly devised IP/TCP Internet host protocol, and as the HOSTS.TXT database became too big to be efficient, the ARPANET was quickly overtaken by the Internet of today. Additionally, the HOSTS.TXT protocol was no longer able to handle the massive load coming from IP-based Internet users, so a new means of connecting users to the Internet through IP addresses had to expand, as well.

At the time, there were a couple of early Internet creators using different name distribution systems. Xerox, for example, had its own, as did Packet

Clearing House. These systems were much too restrictive to accommodate the modern Internet. A new system had to be invented to make life easier for users who wouldn't understand the ins and outs of the Internet. We needed something big but simple and user-friendly.

The Domain Name System to the Rescue?

Symbolics, Inc. was the initial website accessible to users through the DNS. It was the first time that a TLD like the *.com* or *.edu* protocols were utilized. Instead of users needing to know the IP address for Symbolics, they were able to type in the web address — *www.symbolics.com*. It still holds the distinct honor of being the first website registered as part of the new DNS.[2]

From that date until now, hundreds of millions of domain names have been registered. As of the writing of this book, there were more than 370 million TLD names registered with ICANN.[3] Think about this: that number had increased by over three million domain name registrations just from quarter one 2020 to quarter two. That's how massive the growth and how enormous the challenge IT, government, and business professionals face as we try to unlock the best, most efficient way to secure the backbone of the Internet.

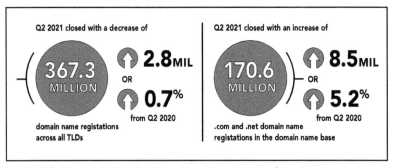

Fig. 3   The Domain Name System registrations *.com* and *.net* continue to increase by millions of records in a year-over-year comparison.

Source: www.verisign.com/en_US/domain-names/dnib/index.xhtml?section=executive-summary,

There were more than 367 million domain names registered across all TLDs by the middle of 2021.[4] Each one is susceptible to the type of attack that could redirect millions of users to malicious sites. A very old and familiar foe to IT security pros is the Mydoom worm. It attacked for the first time in 2004, costing more than $38 billion in damages, and has for years employed simple phishing emails to get users to click on an attachment that infects their systems and then spreads to others in their address books.[5]

Individual users have gotten much more sophisticated about opening phishing emails over the 16 years since Mydoom first appeared, but it still has the capability of doing real damage. Despite being around for nearly two decades, this worm successfully affects 1 percent of its U.S. targets. That's down from 25 percent in 2004, but it's still considered to be perhaps the most dangerous Internet virus to date.

Why the DNS Makes the Internet Scarily Insecure at Its Core

In 2019, a new version of the Mydoom worm attacked the host files for all antivirus and computer security sites, including Microsoft's Windows security updates. This worm affected tens of millions of users and shut down access to websites with the tools and information to stop it.[6] This new version of the old Mydoom worm is circling around the scariest part of the Internet — the host files that populate the DNS.

What the latest attack by Mydoom reminds us of is that the core, the spine, the backbone of the Internet is fundamentally insecure. All of the protections and security laid on top of it don't resolve the underlying problem that the entire Internet is built on a shaky security foundation. To help make the dangers and therefore the solutions crystal-clear, we need to get users, decision-makers, and lawmakers up to speed about the foundation of the DNS and how it operates.

I'm going to make this as simple and painless as possible using the word puzzle analogy in Fig. 2. First, let's define the actors. This would be a good time to take a look at "Essential Terms We Need to Know" near the end of this book to become familiar with some of the components that make up the DNS. But let's start at the most basic part — the hostname files.

The hostname is what we try to get to when we type a web address into the URL. The hostname is the website, the *google* in *www.google.com*. The hostname tells us who owns the site. The website owner applies for use of the domain name, and if approved, the domain as well as the corresponding IP addresses and host files, are added to a registry maintained by ICANN.

Although website owners and hosts don't technically "own" the domain or the domain name, they have exclusive use of it in the same way copyright and trademark law works. However, Internet- and computer-savvy hosts can do real damage, even if unintentionally, as was the case with Verisign's Site Finder a few years ago. Seemingly innocently, the security company used an algorithm that sent any unregistered TLD names under the *.com* or *.net* umbrella to its website. It was stunning to IT security professionals. With that one change, Verisign had, in effect, changed a gigantic chunk of the Internet and limited access for those operating under those unregistered domains or trying to access them.

Even though Verisign has always insisted that it wasn't trying to hurt anything by doing this, the incident did reveal how a small change like that could upend major parts of the backbone of the Internet as we know it. Simply trying to get business from users accessing broken links or unregistered domains by redirecting any query that couldn't be resolved or delivered to its website made the company entity non grata for a while. ICANN had to step in and threaten to revoke Verisign's authority to maintain and administer root nameservers, forcing the company to reverse its changes. This moment in DNS history has sparked the debate and consternation that has led us here today and for people like me to offer solutions that will prevent widespread damage to the Internet.

To fix this problem, we have to get to its root, beginning with the two most important — and dangerous — parts of the DNS: the authority imbued to nameservers and resolvers. This is the area where the types of widespread hacks that keep people like me up at night are most likely to occur.

Getting to the Root of the Problem

Over the next few chapters, I'll delve deeper into the underlying mechanisms of the DNS to provide a solid foundational knowledge of the problem confronting all of us as it pertains to the DNS. For now, I want to start with the bones themselves that make up the spine of the Internet. That begins with the two different lists that constitute the word scramble puzzle in Fig. 2 — the nameservers and resolvers.

Nameservers and Resolvers

In the word puzzle analogy in Fig. 2, the nameserver is the list of images and unscrambled words. The resolver is what figures out the word the user is looking for and connects the two sides, deciphering and then connecting the scrambled word to the unscrambled word. Often these are two separate functions, but a website such as *www.google.com* might combine the resolver function with the nameserver. To do that, there has to be a large cache of information that encompasses every scrambled word on the list and ensures an unscrambled match for each.

The resolvers are an important part of the process. The nameserver is less and less important as routine queries become part of cached data. There's no need to search for the nameserver if the information is already stored locally. And the resolver is good at putting two and two together. Going back to our analogy, the resolver associates the letters *g-o-a-n-e-r* now with fruit and the word *orange*. That's the same as the clues embedded in the resolver's algorithm — clues that give the resolver a head start in its search based on the TLD (*.com*, *.net*, or *.edu*).

The Cache

It sounds like the word *cash* and is actually a good metaphor for what it does. Every local computer, every website, has a cache of data. Some of that data and information is automatically included on a computer when it's power upped for the first time. Most cache data comes from each query made. For instance, in the Fig. 2 word puzzle, now that the resolver has successfully found the image of the orange on the nameserver, that information, that connection, will be stored as cache on that web browser and possibly on the local computer network itself. The next time a search is needed for the image of an orange, the connection to the nameserver has already been established and stored for future use. Now, when *orange* is typed in, the computer doesn't have to search the nameserver or resolve anything — the information is stored in the cache.

The Dangers of Cache Poisoning

One way to tell if a computer is the victim of cache poisoning is if the Internet slows way down on it. The faster a computer can connect from a query to the website, the faster the overall Internet is. Viruses that infect local computers and spy on users' browsing histories are looking for cached data. Cache is important to maintain because users are less likely to be directed to broken links or to get error messages when queries are performed.

Before the DNS, the error rates if the website wasn't exactly typed correctly were on average between 20 and 60 percent, hugely inefficient and one of the reasons why the DNS using nameservers and resolvers became the standard solution. There had to be a way to account for small errors that would still lead users to websites they were trying to access. Website administrators would attempt to create lists of words that users might search and account for spelling errors, but it still produced high error rates and undeliverable messages, only reducing errors by 10 percent and averaging error rates in one out of four queries.

So the importance of caching data can easily be seen as necessary for the Internet to function smoothly. Cache and nameservers can now recognize that the problem might be user error and not a missing website, so Google, for example, will correct a query, asking, "Did you mean …?" That has cleaned up those high error rates and made the DNS and the Internet overall much more efficient. But there's a deeper, a great deal more sinister way that the cache can be used to disrupt and possibly destroy large swaths of the Internet.

Since 2008, we've seen cache-poisoning attacks of increasing severity that have the ability to shut down large DNS servers. AT&T that year was the victim of hackers who attacked its DNS servers with cache poisoning.[7] As recently as 2018, Amazon was the victim of a cache-poisoning assault that redirected its users to a malicious website. So far the damage has been to users of these specific websites. Employing some of the data stored in cache files, these malicious actors are able to interrupt the line connecting *goaner* to *orange* and intercepting it and then redirecting it not just to the wrong word but a bad word that can infect a personal computer and those connected to it.

Now imagine what would happen if hackers were able to figure out a way to burn down that connection altogether, to get in there and delete all the cache on the unscrambled list and replace it with a bunch of ransomware sites. Just think what a large-scale attack like that on Google, Facebook, or Amazon would do to the Internet as a whole. That's one of the many night-mare scenarios this book will attempt to prevent with smart, well-thought-out solutions to the DNS problem created by ARPANET's Achilles' heel.

Truth in Domain Names Act

Power struggles between countries, companies, and organizations tend to cloud the debate over what to do about the yawning insecurity of the DNS that I've described. So far those discussions have only resulted in half measures and solutions that fall well short of the fundamental problem. Nonetheless, there have been changes to the system through legislation aimed at controlling certain aspects of the DNS with limited success.

Since the turn of the 21st century, the need for more security to protect users online has increasingly become apparent. In the early part of the decade, catfishing and sex trafficking online became such a problem that in 2003 the United States enacted the Truth in Domain Names Act. That law, as well as the PROTECT Act, put restrictions on how websites can use their domain names to attract certain users to their websites by forbidding the use of misleading names that could attract minors to a porn site, for example. Clearly, laws like that were and are still needed, but they still don't get at the core insecurities and vulnerabilities of the DNS.

PART TWO

DNS —
THE SECURITY
VULNERABILITIES
OF THE DNS

HACKERS
ARE SEIZING
THE MOMENT

DNS
SECURITY

4

Crash Course in Current DNS Security

A Quick Tour of the DNS

Before we get into DNS security challenges and solutions over the next four chapters, here's a quick tour of the DNS to solidify the concepts defined in "Essential Terms We Need to Know" near the end of this book. By doing a search for my website, *www.craigmackinder.com*, we can see how all the operations come together.

Every DNS server on the Internet will query another server above *www.craigmackinder.com* in the namespace if it doesn't have the information required. It might try to look up *www.craigmackinder.com* to find the address of the server hosting my website. Generally speaking, though, here's what a computer does to find it.

Assuming that the ISP is Comcast and the computer has been automatically configured by that company to use its DNS servers to resolve Internet names, after *www.craigmackinder.com* is typed into the browser, here's what the request would be in six steps:

1. "Hey, Comcast DNS servers, where can I find *www.craigmackinder.com?*"

2. Comcast's DNS servers then check their list of recently accessed websites. Alas, very few visitors ever request this information, so Comcast's DNS servers don't have the answer in their caches.

3. Comcast's DNS servers talk to the .(*root*) providers to find out which servers host the .*com DNS* records. Comcast's DNS servers are referred by IP address to query the .*com DNS* servers next.

4. Comcast's DNS servers talk to the .com providers to find out which servers host www.craigmackinder.com. They're referred to the DNS hosting providers for www.craigmackinder.com at DNS All Stars.

5. Comcast's DNS servers talk to the dnsallstars.com servers to find out if there's a record for www.craigmackinder.com. DNS All Stars servers reply with the IP address for the server hosting www.craigmackinder.com.

6. The computer web browser then connects to the server hosting www.craigmackinder.com and requests the website www.craigmackinder.com where at last my website is found.

Reading these steps takes a hundred times longer than a computer runs through all of them. In fact, this all happens in a matter of seconds, and now that *www.craigmackinder.com* is stored in a user's cache, the next time it should only take a split second to get to my website from the user's IP address.

When a computer user registers *my-fantastic-new-business.com*, he or she is buying the services of the root *(.root)* servers, the TLD servers, and the user's domain registrar servers. They all need to be employed to work well and function all the time for customers to reach a new website.

DNS Security Is Moving to the Forefront

Hacks like the ones that hit Target on Black Friday in 2013 sent ripples through the general public.[1] Was user information safe? Who had their credit card information? What if their identities were stolen? Not even a year later, North Korea stopped the presses when a hack from that country shut down movie production at Sony.[2] Those large-scale attacks that grabbed headlines started with a simple phishing email, or a saboteur installing a flash drive in a network computer. Businesses and IT security professionals alike began to beef up their systems to prepare for more attacks of that kind in the future. But something happened in 2008 that sent shockwaves through the IT security community. Our worst fears were realized — someone or something had figured out a way to attack the DNS.

Today, DNS poisoning of the kind that IT security writer Dan Kaminsky alerted the world to in 2008 has become one of the most common DNS attack techniques.[3] It's able to fill the cache of a nameserver with junk or malicious data so that any query looking for a particular website or searching under a specific term receives an erroneous response. Resolvers have no way of detecting junk data from real data. Because the DNS is totally unencrypted and the entire system relies on making the correct connection from query to retrieval, the inability of recursive resolvers to determine if information contained in those cache files is correct creates a huge gap in the fundamental security of the Internet.

Up until now, big headline-grabbing hacks at the end of the day almost always led back to a phishing email or a flash drive surreptitiously installed on a computer. Most hackers rely on user error or an inside person. These new attacks on the DNS require no such thing. In fact, DNS attacks work when users access a known, typically safe website. In 2019, the FBI sent out alerts warning businesses, governments, telecoms, and ISPs about a string of DNS attacks that were taking shape.[4] What's most noticeable about these assaults is that they're getting more sophisticated and harder to detect.

There are ways to secure valid certifications from the agencies that issue transport layer security (TLS) certificates, and there have even been attacks on the registrars themselves. There's so much damage that can be done with certificates and valid access to resolvers that DNSpionage agents can go well beyond shutting down movie production. These hackers can collect usernames, passwords, personal information, and business and government information on a scale we've never seen before, all without being detected. DNS hijackers have seized control of entire domains on several continents, including North America.

Why isn't the 2008 DNS attack more widely known? I argue that most people using the Internet really don't understand how it works. Comprehending this problem requires greater Internet literacy not just from users but from decision-makers, as well, which is the motivation for this book. Knowing is half the battle. In that sense, there's some good news. With the volume and types of DNS attacks increasing right now, businesses and governments everywhere are beginning to treat this threat with the seriousness it deserves. There's actually a menu of DNS attacks now that can be identified that will help guide everyone involved to the best solutions for securing the DNS.

Most Common Types of DNS Attacks

Once upon a time, meaning a few years ago, the most prolific and dangerous assault on the DNS was the DDoS attack, which literally means distributed denial of service, computer jargon for flooding a DNS server with queries. Hackers use bots and malware to send millions of requests to look up information on the Internet at the same time so that it overwhelms the DNS servers supporting those requests. One such strike in 2016 knocked Twitter out for millions of users on the U.S. East Coast by attacking DNS nameservers in the same region (see Fig. 4).

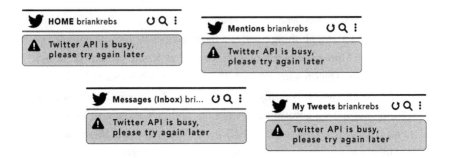

Fig. 4 Twitter afflicted with problems in 2016, as witnessed in the social media platform Hootsuite.
Source: https://krebsonsecurity.com/2016/10/ddos-on-dyn-impacts-twitter-spotify-reddit.

Compared to the DNS incursions we're seeing of late, DDoS offensives like the one that temporarily took down Twitter are starting to look somewhat quaint. Before we get into the next chapters covering solutions, it's important to know the types of DNS attacks that are known as of now and how they work. What follows is a rundown of the most prevalent and dangerous ones that have happened over the past few years and months.

Cache Attacks: Attacking Stored Data on Servers

There are a couple of known DNS assaults that target caches on computers, web browsers, and DNS servers. As pointed out in "Essential Terms We Need to Know" near the end of this book, cache is data stored every time something is looked up on the Internet. An ISP uses servers that contain cache data, a computer caches data automatically, and browsers that can be accessed often collect data and store it in cache files.

Cache Poisoning or Spoofing

This type of attack happens when cache files on a public server, an ISP's server, or a computer user's cache files have had malicious IP addresses or domain names secretly put into them.[5] Once fake or spoofed IP addresses and/or domain names are in cache files, when a legitimate query for that data is made, instead of correctly connecting to *orange*, malware diverts the request for *orange* to a *bushel of poisonous apples*. There is malware capable of filling cache files with unauthorized entries into the DNS. Resolvers simply add the new IP addresses and are unable to discern between real and fake ones (see Fig. 5).

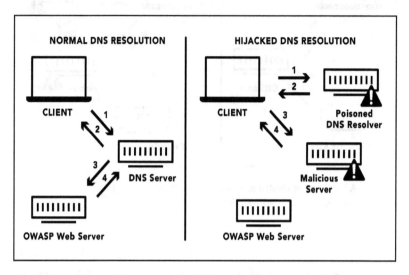

Fig. 5   A topological illustration of a DNS cache-poisoning attack.
Source: https://owasp.org/www-chapter-ghana/assets/slides/DNS_Cache_Poisoning(OWASP_GHANA).pdf.

Server Attacks: Direct Attacks on DNS Servers

Perhaps for IT professionals, the most dangerous and scary DNS attacks we've seen are the ones that attempt to go right at the fundamental stability of the Internet. These are direct attacks on nameservers at the highest levels, including DNSpionage by nation-states.

DNS Hijacking

This attack might seem like spoofing, but it's even more sinister. Instead of planting errant IP addresses in cache files, a DNS hijacking literally hijacks the domain of a particular website. For instance, when a user tries to get to Amazon's website, a DNS hijacking changes the actual listing of that domain's IP address within the DNS records kept by the authoritative agencies. So, to users, it seems as if they've landed on the legitimate Amazon website but instead they're on a fake malicious website. Now imagine how many purchases could be made by legitimate customers without them even suspecting they've handed all their credit card information over to nefarious hackers (see Fig. 6).

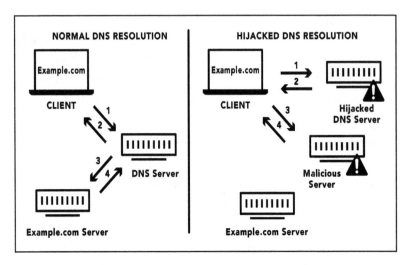

Fig. 6 A topological illustration of DNS hijacking.
Source: www.cloudflare.com/learning/dns/dns-security.

Tunneling

Hackers using DNS tunneling go through DNS protocols to disrupt queries. They're able to sneak malware into websites by trolling through popular queries and then redirecting users through the *http* protocol or the TCP protocol, which are different segments of each URL address that users type into a browser. By doing it this way, hackers are able to get around firewalls that would prevent this kind of hack.

NXDOMAIN DNS Attacks

Similar to a typical DDoS assault, NXDOMAIN DNS attacks flood DNS servers with requests, but in this one, the requests are for websites and domains that don't exist. It ties up the resolvers trying to find the requested IP addresses as well as knots up the numerous servers that are accessed to find the answer to the query. Similar to cache poisoning, it exploits cache but at the resolver level and doesn't fill it with malicious IP addresses. Rather, it generates more garbage requests that clog up resolvers. An attack on the right root server can knock out an entire swath of the Internet.

DNS Subdomain Attacks

Individual corporations and government entities are becoming all too familiar with DNS subdomain attacks, which are direct hits on specific websites or domains. These are DDoS assaults directed at base nameservers for specific domains. So, if attackers wanted to shut down Amazon, they would send requests for subdomains that don't exist under Amazon's nameserver — in essence, shutting the website down by preventing legitimate traffic from reaching the website while its server is tied up retrieving random nonexistent queries sent by the attacker's malware.

Resolver Attacks: Attacking the DNS Recursive Resolver

Every time a web address or search word is typed in and enter is hit, a query is created. Initially, that query or question goes to a local server, typically the user's ISP one. But once the query leaves a local server, where does it go? The first stop is the default server for the Internet called the DNS "recursive" resolver server.[6] Think of it as the master list. As such, it maintains queries and cache files for gigantic portions of the Internet. Because of that, the time to live (TTL) is very important to understand.

There are time limits on nearly all queries for how long they'll be cached or stored. The resolver also has access to the DNS root server, which if disrupted, could cause immeasurable damage. Resolvers also retrieve authoritative nameservers when looking up queries that again, in the hands of the wrong entity, could disrupt the Internet in unimaginable ways. Naturally, as big as the recursive resolver is, it doesn't hang on to most queries for very long, but for some it does. DNS saboteurs realize this and are finding new and inventive ways to attack resolvers.

Phantom DNS Attacks

Phantom attacks in the grand scheme of things aren't benign but not nearly as lethal as some of the other DNS assaults we've seen. As with the NXDOMAIN attack, servers are flooded with requests, but in this intrusion, the resolvers look up queries by accessing phony domain servers that have been set up and are controlled by saboteurs. These fake servers don't even bother to respond to resolver requests or respond so slowly that the result is a DDoS for anyone accessing information through those servers.

Domain Lockup

Another attack on the resolvers happens when bad actors create their own dummy domains with phony resolvers that connect to real resolvers. That way they can siphon off legitimate requests going to real resolvers, slowing them down and hence causing a traffic jam for those particular resolvers.

Registrar Attacks: Attacking the Internet's Infrastructure

In Chapter 2, I talked about the organizations that control the Internet. One of the biggest and most important entities helping to maintain the Internet's stability is the Packet Clearing House. In February 2019, PCH had to issue a public acknowledgment that indeed hackers were able to compromise the entity charged with maintaining the domain name registration database for the entire Internet.[7]

DNSpionage agents used phishing emails to access credentials that enabled them to send a message globally to registrars about legitimate changes to domain names, records, and registrations. It's called the extensible provisioning protocol (EPP), and until 2019, largely only registrars and IT professionals knew it existed. The EPP is used by registrars to securely and privately update domain information. Hackers were able to steal credentials that gave them access to the EPP interface used by the Internet's registrars. Because only those in the know have access to EPP commands, they're usually instituted without question. The hackers were unable to send the correct commands and therefore weren't able to do lasting damage, but clearly it's only a matter of time. The damage that could be done by hackers with the keys to the entire DNS registration command protocol could be devastating.

ISP Attacks: Attacking Local ISP Servers and the Internet of Things (IoT)

Customer Premise Equipment (CPE) Attacks

ISPs provide not only local DNS servers to their customers but also typically their equipment such as routers and modems. Cable boxes today are also tied to the Internet and are connected to ISP servers so that any attacks on them can spread like wildfire for individual home-based users. Either through malware or on-premise sabotage, customer premise equipment (CPE) attackers are able to siphon information from devices to conduct strikes on targeted websites and domains under the radar.

Google has given users a free workaround by sharing a public resolver address. Instead of users' ISP server resolvers handling queries, if routers are changed to the 8.8.8.8 Google resolver, Google takes care of queries instead of Comcast, for example.

DNS Authorities Attacks

An industrious DNSpionage agent has started a new attack vector in DNS security — authoritative agencies. Like the attacks on registrars that go to the heart of the Internet's infrastructure, cybercriminals have recently set their sights on botnets to assault DNS authorities such as PCH and Dyn (an Internet performance management and web application security company). Using a combination of ransomware and DNS attacks, these cyber extortionists demand bitcoins in exchange for releasing or not deleting parts of the DNS infrastructure.

Original Design of the DNS Completely Overlooked Security

In hindsight, there were two reasons why the original design of the DNS didn't account for security vulnerabilities. It might seem foolish now, but frankly, the Internet's creators were aware of the potential for bad actors to usurp user data and invade privacy. There were even signs that the DNS from the beginning was going to miss a crucial security feature — encryption. But the need for the Internet to grow and expand unfettered weighed more heavily.

Dozens of attack vectors were inadvertently produced simply because the originators understood that for this technology to become what it is today — grow freely and unfettered — there had to be distributed control. There could be no single operating system controlled by a particular company that all other users on any given network would have to mimic architecturally. For one thing, it would make adoption of the Internet too expensive. The goal was to keep the Internet as unrestrained as possible and to prevent unitary control of any part of it.

That meant that browser owners couldn't initiate their own encryption tools for queries because those websites wouldn't necessarily be compatible with all the other browsers on the Internet. That left all queries unencrypted to keep the Internet lean while enabling the underlying distributed database to develop without any kind of restraints.[9] As such, every website could communicate using the common language of the DNS, which in turn would increase the dynamism and functionality of the expanding Internet, but security concerns weren't part of that discussion:

> The "leanness" criterion led to a conscious decision to omit many
> of the functions one might expect in a state-of-the-art database. In
> particular, dynamic update of the database with the related atomicity,

voting, and backup considerations was omitted. The intent was to add these eventually, but it was believed that a system that included these features would be viewed as too complex to be accepted by the community.[10]

Another glaring problem that almost everyone involved in the early implementation of the Internet recognized was the limitation of data type and class versus their growth. The types of data and the different classification categories to sort them by were too limited, most people thought. Many believed it should be at least three times bigger to allow for classes and types to be expanded as new Internet technologies came into being. Instead, for the first five years of the Internet's existence, there were only two additions to data types and only two new classes added, while two types were dropped:

> While one problem is that almost all existing software regards types and classes as compile-time constants, and hence requires recompilation to deal with changes, a less tractable problem is that new data types and classes are useless until their semantics are carefully designed and published, applications created to use them, and a consensus is reached to use the new system across the Internet. This means that new types face a series of technical and political hurdles.[11]

Back in 1992 there were less than 10 data classes and types. Since then, several more record types have been added, but there's still a great deal of effort and argument that happens to this day during the process of adding new data types and classes. Looking back at the original DNS design, it's clear that these underlying security omissions in the beginning would have been much easier to fix. However, when you consider just how much effort goes into adding a few new class or data types, it's obvious why making a fundamental change to the underlying structure and architecture of the DNS is going to take a very well-considered solution.

When you realize that it took a decade and a half after the Internet first went live for a hacker to send out the first virus, it makes sense why security wasn't at the forefront of the Internet creators' minds. Businesses and individuals were more interested in being able to get online and use the Internet than worrying about security threats to their data. In the early days, the most data any hacker could get would be email addresses and web comments, but no real personal information. Today, it's all too apparent just how rife the Internet is with extremely sensitive and valuable private personal, government, and corporate data and why DNS security has to be at the forefront now.

It's Time for a Redesign of the DNS

So far this discussion of DNS security has been somewhat abstract, but an attack in 2014 helps illustrate the stark reality of the situation. Turkey conducted what has been coined an "on-path-attacker" assault on the DNS against its own citizens.[12] In an effort to quash dissent in its country, the Turkish government intercepted queries going to Twitter from ISPs inside Turkey and redirected them to the government's website. One thing became quickly apparent after this incident: there has to be greater control over authentication among the naming authorities for the DNS.

As explained in "Essential Terms We Need to Know" near the end of this book, governments are one of the few entities granted some control over their registered TLDs. They're still overseen by the authorities at ICANN, but governments with control over their TLDs, like Turkey's, do have the power to redirect traffic through their local servers, since ICANN doesn't authenticate the legitimacy of those modifications in such cases.

Fig. 7 During Turkey's blocking of Twitter using its own DNS, graffiti sprang up around the country to inform citizens about Google's 8.8.8.8 recursive resolver, which they could get use to access Twitter.
Source: hhttps://blog.cloudflare.com/dnssec-an-introduction.

The second thing the Turkish example underscores is the potential for nation-states to attack other nation-states in the same manner. A nation-state known for its cyber assaults on other countries, such as North Korea, might infiltrate foreign ISPs, intercept queries going to Twitter, and redirect those queries to another source to disseminate its propaganda and misinformation. However, Turkish citizens were able to get around their government's shutdown of Twitter. The free Google recursive resolver address, 8.8.8.8, popped up spray-painted on buildings throughout the country, thwarting Turkey's ability to block the social media site (see Fig. 7).

Still, it didn't take IT security professionals long to run worst-case scenarios for these kinds of DNS attacks. And the problem is growing, specifically in the Middle East. According to research published by *KrebsOnSecurity*, in 2019, there were a variety of DNS attacks going after different parts of the system in more than 50 different countries and companies in the Middle East.[13] Worse, these same hackers aimed their sights on two of the most important credentialing authorities for the Internet — Netnod Internet Exchange and Packet Clearing House.

Once hackers are able to authenticate credentials within nameservers, root servers, or registrars, the door is wide open for extremely damaging attacks on large parts of the Internet. Netnod, based in Sweden, is a registrar and one of the 13 root servers undergirding the Internet. Parts of the Netnod DNS infrastructure were hijacked by hackers in December 2018 and January 2019. PCH, a nonprofit that manages a significant amount of the world's DNS infrastructure, was hit with the same kind of DNS strike just prior to the Netnod attack, giving bad actors access to two other registrars where they were able to change records within the DNS for both Netnod and PCH.[14]

As the overseer for all the most used and popular 500 TLDs, PCH is a crucial component for maintaining the stability of the Internet and as such is an extremely critical vulnerability in overall DNS security. For this reason alone, it's long past time for a redesign of the authorities, credentialing, and authentication of the DNS. A major solution to this problem is very local DNS. Still, for a solution that will keep the Internet free and nimble yet fundamentally secure, it will require all parties involved, from users, to open Internet advocates, to governments, to corporations.

5

The DNS Threat Assessment

July 2020 saw something happen to Cloudflare similar to what Verisign experienced in the early 2000s. A major Internet security firm with ties to some of the world's biggest commercial providers, Cloudflare caused a blackout that hit its global traffic in an instant.[1] The company was trying to perform a routine update, but something went wrong, and instead of updating, it caused a super-traffic jam in one of Cloudflare's post office protocol (POP) servers. Large corporations that count on Cloudflare's technology to block DDoS attacks were left unprotected while the Cloudflare servers remained down and one DNS provider's website went black, as well. The damage that could have been done by a simple mistake in an update to the DNS could have caused enormous harm to corporations.

Not only is the DNS completely unencrypted but threats to it come from everywhere, with some bad actors targeting its core vulnerabilities. On top of that, threat vectors are expanding. Instead of simply trying to disrupt queries, DNS hackers endeavor to black out and/or block huge chunks of the Internet for money and other nefarious reasons. Attacks have spread from public Wi-Fi hotspots down to mobile network operators (MNOs).[2]

One DNS security provider breaks down DNS threats to corporations into two different buckets.[3] First, hackers attacking individual company nameservers attempt to shut down those corporations, which includes assaults on registry operators (ROs), naming agencies, and web hosts, among others. The goal here is to destroy a specific entity despite the likelihood of collateral damage like that seen after Cloudflare's botched update. Second, the attacks are similar to the PCH and Dyn ones discussed in the previous chapter. The target isn't a business but the authorities governing the DNS and a company's servers. In this case, the collateral damage is intended on the way to the real target — the root servers.

For corporations operating in cyberspace, there's a sort of mutually assured destruction with their online customers. Severe attacks and breaches not only result in tens of millions of dollars in damages but the trust lost from consumers usually causes users to avoid those websites altogether or at the very least stops them from putting any of their personal identification information on that particular website in the future. In turn, businesses lose customers and money on top of the costs of repairing the breach.

For DNS attacks, the damage could be existential, and yet, based on research by the Ponemon Institute, corporations are woefully unequipped to handle this threat.[4] Ponemon's data shows that corporations are missing the threat in five major ways:

- They're unprepared for DNS threats.
- They show big gaps in monitoring threats.
- Their threat assessments are too focused on exfiltration.
- Their threat investigations are inadequate.
- They lack dedicated personnel focused on DNS security.

Raids against the DNS have happened against all kinds of entities, from hospital networks and government systems to giant corporations and personal home computers. The threat, if it hadn't been before, is now clear and present. The solution to the problem will involve all players. Big business and corporations have a crucial role to play in securing the DNS. However, not all corporations are fully aware of the threat, and as research conducted by the Ponemon Institute in 2018 shows, too few are prepared to handle it.

Dissecting the DNS Threat Assessment from the Ponemon Institute

The amount of data coursing through the DNS is staggering to think about. Traffic between IP addresses on an annual basis is expected to top three zettabytes in 2022. The reach of that data has expanded well beyond the Internet type and includes billions of devices connected to the IoT, which is expected to reach 125 billion devices over the next decade. The challenge we all face is to secure that data in an environment where the standard malware attacks the world has come to expect grew to 780 million different ones between 2010 and 2020. That's despite all the different kinds of Internet security tools developed to thwart those attacks.

As if that wasn't a big enough challenge, after surveying more than 1,000 professionals working in IT and IT security from the United States, Europe, the Middle East, and Africa about DNS risks, researchers at the Ponemon Institute concluded that worldwide "most organizations are underprepared to deal with security issues."[5] Based on the DNS Risk Index calculated in conjunction with Infoblox, which compiled the score from 24 questions, the global risk to the DNS is 57 percent.

Corporations Are Unprepared for DNS Threats

Corporations make up the vast majority of the 500 top-level dot-com domains on the Internet. These websites are among some of the most lucrative and are part of the vast global e-commerce market. A huge disruption to dot-com root servers would have a devastating effect on individual corporations, yes, but also on global commerce as a whole. The Ponemon Institute identifies several areas where corporations are underprepared for the threats to the DNS.

Top of the list of places corporations are missing the ball is in the architecture of their security systems. Most operate from an IT security perspective that's becoming outdated year by year. For the majority of businesses, their security architecture isn't prepared to handle new and evolving threats. Researchers have identified a lack of end-to-end visibility of DNS security threats and that a lot of businesses aren't tracking all the assets in their networks that could provide attack vectors. By the numbers, the study shows:

- *Sixty-four percent say there's no consolidated view of all their physical, virtual, and cloud assets to give a clear picture of the networks' overall threat landscape. The majority of those surveyed noted they rely on DNS data (52 percent) to alert them to assets that might be compromised. And those that do consolidate threat information typically have to put together data from different programs to come up with a full picture.*

- *Fifty-three percent use data gathered from their DNS firewalls to mitigate and protect data from malware, yet only 26 percent have implemented the latest firewall technology that includes monitoring traffic going to and from DNS servers to safeguard company data.*

- *Forty-six percent of those surveyed said they neither identify nor track IoT devices, endpoints, servers, or virtual reality (VR) tools as they're added to their networks. Those that do track new assets use archaic and inefficient means to do so: 39 percent employ spreadsheets to track new assets, 39 percent depend on polling, and 38 percent rely on detection software to track new assets.*

- **Forty-five percent** of those surveyed say their companies implement DNS service providers for all their DNS management, including threat management and mitigation. Only 40 percent manage attacks themselves within the company by monitoring huge upticks in traffic to their servers.

- **Forty-four percent** do audits from time to time. As Ponemon researchers point out, manual audits are full of human error, are terribly inefficient, and take too long to complete to be useful.

- **Thirty-seven percent** of those surveyed say they have no answer for DNS server attacks. At best, companies generally record where hits are coming from, the types of DNS attacks they are, patterns in the types of attacks so they can understand them, yet they have no real solution for handling or preventing them.[6]

Finally, the last percentage above shows just how yesterday a few years ago is in terms of Internet security. Seventy-five percent of those surveyed by the Ponemon Institute utilize an antivirus as well as endpoint security to detect and thwart hackers attempting to access malicious domains through their corporate servers. Maybe five years ago, 75 percent would be an impressive number, but it proves that corporations are set up to prevent malware attacks of the past but not at all prepared to thwart DNS attacks of the kind we're seeing today.[7]

Corporations Show Big Gaps in Threat Monitoring

If corporations aren't getting the full picture of all the threats coming at them, there are going to be gaps in threat monitoring. The vast majority, 75 percent of respondents, use feeds from the government and trusted Internet security professionals to keep an eye on incoming threats. US-CERT, for example, is a private-public partnership that employs both government and private-sector IT professionals to help monitor global threats.[8] It's definitely helpful to subscribe to feeds like this to bolster overall threat monitoring, but it is incredibly inefficient as a sole source for monitoring global threats to the DNS. Yet:

- **Fifty-two percent** of those surveyed employ a mix of free open-source threat feeds, government-threat feeds, other commercial threat feeds, and their own internal threat feeds to monitor incoming threats.

- **Thirty-four percent** *use primarily free open-source threat feeds and blacklists to monitor incoming threats.*

- **Sixteen percent** *rely on just one threat feed from a commercial source.*[9]

The Ponemon survey found that even when corporations consolidate threat data from multiple sources (45 percent), that information isn't appropriately shared throughout their organizations. In fact, 42 percent of those surveyed say that while they utilize multiple threat feeds to monitor threats, that information is parceled out and segregated from different departments or areas of specialty. Only 29 percent distribute consolidated threat information among all their IT security personnel. Regardless, this type of threat monitoring does nothing to stop or prevent DNS attacks.[10]

Corporate Threat Assessments Are Too Focused Primarily on Exfiltration

Particularly in research, data exfiltration is a real threat. That's when malware or even an on-site saboteur hacks into a network and siphons off data. While it's a real threat for businesses of all types, corporations are far more focused on this threat than on DNS-based attacks that can do irrevocable damage to their organizations. The numbers bear this out:

- **Fifty-four percent** *of those surveyed by the Ponemon Institute say that DNS-based exfiltration is a big worry for their organizations.*

- **Fifty percent** *encrypt their data in order to prevent data exfiltration through the DNS.*

- **Forty percent** *utilize endpoint security software to prevent data exfiltration.*[11]

These worries aren't unfounded. Infoblox reported on a recent survey covering DNS security that revealed 46 percent of those polled had been hit with data exfiltration.[12] Another 45 percent were victims of DNS tunneling — an attack applied specifically to siphon off data. Respondents place such a high importance on data exfiltration monitoring because it's so hard to detect, prevent, or recover from.

At the same time, Ponemon's researchers found that less than 20 percent of IT professionals surveyed use a threat detection tool that specifically monitors DNS-based exfiltration.[13] So the fact that the standard firewalls and endpoint security apparatuses that have to date been used as major components of corporate Internet security demonstrates that DNS attackers are finding simple ways to get around those components. The focus has to be on DNS security for all IT teams.

Corporate Threat Investigations Are Inadequate

Believe it or not, in the digital age we live in, most threat investigations, according to the Ponemon Institute, are done manually for the most part. Just barely more than half of the respondents to the aforementioned survey (52 percent) say they perform their own threat investigations, while 42 percent rely on searching through information manually to discover threats. Moreover, the features that are most important to corporations for preventing DNS-based attacks, according to the survey, miss the mark entirely.

As you can see from Fig. 8, reducing false positives when monitoring DNS threats is ranked highest among respondents. At the bottom, at only 28 percent, is "the ability to integrate big data analytics to achieve greater visibility and precision in the intelligence-gathering and dissemination process." Those numbers should be completely inverted. Digging even deeper, 71 percent say the reduction of false positives is "critical."[14]

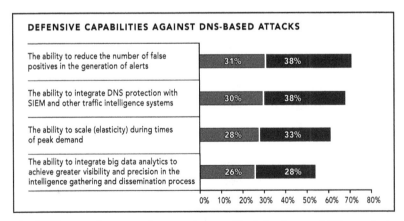

Fig. 8 The most important features that provide defensive capabilities against DNS-based attacks.

Source: www.infoblox.com/wp-content/uploads/infoblox-whitepaper-assessing-the-dns-security-risk.pdf.

When these two ideas are factored together, it's easy to see why corporate threat investigations are so inadequate. Corporations concentrate on the wrong things to shore up their DNS servers, while at the same time they conduct threat investigations manually and rely on others to share attack information. For a real solution to work, corporate leaders have to get up to speed with actual threats to their security in 2021 and beyond rather than what might have worked five years ago.

Corporations Lack Dedicated Personnel Focused on DNS Security

Finally and perhaps most importantly, there has to be dedicated personnel in every organization focused squarely on DNS security. It can no longer be a part of the overall IT department's security infrastructure or a side note in an executive meeting. The DNS is so large and complex that it requires teams concentrated on mitigating these types of attacks in addition to all the other threats corporate IT departments have dealt with for years.

According to the Ponemon Institute's research, the majority of businesses work without a team focused on thwarting DNS attacks and securing DNS servers:

- *Sixty-seven percent* spread DNS security responsibilities among multiple teams.

- *Fifty-eight percent* lack dedicated personnel covering DNS security or spread the responsibility among other teams.

- *Thirty-two percent* have no one and no team dedicated to securing DNS servers.[15]

Generally speaking, most corporations opt to farm out these duties to IT security firms. Among those surveyed, 63 percent employ Cisco, Akamai, Infoblox, or BlueCat to manage their DNS security. Nearly half of those responding use cloud service providers to manage their DNS and to mitigate attacks. DNS cloud providers are a smart option for companies without in-house expertise to manage threats. Still, corporations have to place a much stronger emphasis on DNS threat monitoring and mitigation. Having dedicated personnel within IT departments committed solely to managing DNS in conjunction with a DNS cloud provider is the best solution.[16]

6

DNS Security Vulnerabilities and the Impact on Internet Infrastructure

The Largest DDoS Attack Ever

Early in the morning of October 21, 2016, the United States experienced the largest DDoS attack in history. There were several novel features of this assault that sparked the urgency we're seeing today to guard the DNS. For instance, the attack was directed right at one of the authorities governing the DNS — Dyn — which plays a hugely important role in maintaining and securing the DNS's infrastructure. By attacking Dyn, the hackers were able to knock out many different popular websites in the United States, basically shutting down a huge region of the Internet all day. Among the victims of this attack were:

- Airbnb.
- *Boston Globe*.
- Github.
- *New York Times*.
- Reddit.
- Shopify.
- SoundCloud.
- Spotify.
- Twitter.
- Vox.[1]

Another freaky and frankly frightening part about this attack is that it increased in size just weeks after what was initially the largest DDoS blitz in history when hackers targeted cybersecurity expert and writer Brian Krebs of *KrebsOnSecurity*.[2] They used the same novel technique discovered in the

Krebs hit: a botnet to compromise IoT devices (CCTV, routers, security cameras, DVRs, et cetera), thus increasing the size of the assault. Botnets typically come from a network of malicious computers sending millions of packets of junk data to servers to crash them. The Mirai botnet that struck Krebs was the first to target the DNS through a botnet that enlisted IoT devices.

Expanding the attack's reach to the IoT created 100,000 vectors that increased the strength of the offensive to historic proportions at 1.2 Tbps (terabytes per second or a trillion bytes per second).[3] This is double the size of any previous incursion of its kind ever. It also revealed just how dangerous an attack like this can be considering how insecure IoT devices are combined with how many there are in the world — roughly five times the number of users there are on the planet. As one expert added, "Imagine what a well-resourced state actor could do with insecure IoT devices."

Shortly after the Krebs attack, code for the Mirai botnet that spread so rapidly was posted online. Since then, these assaults have become ever-increasing in size and ferocity. It's clear that by attacking Dyn and other authorities in conjunction with security experts and firms that help combat these types of raids, hackers have figured out ways to sustain attacks by shutting down the agencies, companies, and organizations in charge of maintaining the Internet as well as those charged with protecting it.

Largely aimed at the United States, the attack against Dyn is an ominous sign of what's to come if DNS security vulnerabilities persist. As the spokesperson for Dyn put it, "It's so distributed, coming from tens of millions of source IP addresses around the world."[4] After Dyn shut down the first attack at nine in the morning on October 21, another wave hit. Before that one could be dealt with, another one struck. It took most of the day before Dyn was able to stop that attack.

Free Wi-Fi is also being exploited, providing DNS hackers with public inroads into the DNS.[5] It can happen from anywhere, and with botnets like Mirai, it's become much easier and cost-effective to conduct ever-expanding DNS attacks. While the assault on Dyn is considered the largest successful DDoS strike in history, Amazon Web Services was able to fight back and prevent an attack in February 2020 nearly twice the size of the Dyn one.[6]

DNSpionage Is Increasing in Danger

In November 2018, Cisco coined the term *DNSpionage* to describe a massive attack on DNS servers in Lebanon and the United Arab Emirates (UAE).[7]

This was no ordinary attack; it was a DNS hijacking. The haul was impressively disconcerting. The hijackers took control of the DNS servers for those two countries, as well as those of several private businesses, and redirected IP traffic to a malicious site.

During the time the hijackers had control of those servers, they were able to secure encryption certificates that allowed them to steal email passwords and logins as well as decrypt traffic accessing servers through company VPNs, enabling them to not just intercept those emails but to read them.

The scariest part about this story is that it was only the beginning. In fact, based on research by FireEye reported in January 2019, it was an ongoing attack that started in late 2017.[8] DNSpionage has only been increasing since then, and the vast majority of hacks are now aimed at DNS attack vectors. According to Infoblox, 90 percent of malware and ransomware strikes target DNS infrastructure, which only increases the urgency to shore up DNS security vulnerabilities.[9]

DNS's Vulnerabilities to IP Discovery

IP addresses — the things that make the Internet go — are an extremely vulnerable attack vector. It's where traffic is intercepted and how cache poisoning is pulled off. And it's increasingly the means to get into the DNS's core vulnerabilities. Hackers try to discover IP addresses that can be utilized to exploit the underpinnings of the Internet. Over the past several years as these attacks have increased, Cloudflare has identified the various methods by which hackers attempt to discover IP addresses to pull off bigger and more devastating attacks. What follows is a rundown of the most common IP discovery methods and how they work.[10]

The "Direct-Connect" Subdomain Approach

This technique attempts to uncover IP addresses by searching through the leaves of the tree along its branches. In other words, for each TLD where there's a subdomain that has access to the server, when a query is made, the subdomain reveals the web server's IP address. Although most online users know nothing about this or which specific "direct-connect" subdomain of Cloudflare is being exploited to discover IP addresses, hackers do. Cloudflare has since randomized this subdomain, but older systems are still vulnerable to this approach.

IP Discovery Through MX Servers

MX servers are tied to an email exchange. Most of the time, company email servers are a part of the main server. MX records contained in that server provide access to the web server where IP addresses can be discovered using a simple query. Having a separate server for email exchanges, or using a third party to provide email services, can prevent this type of IP discovery. However, most email exchanges are hosted on the same network and web server.

IP Discovery Through a Websocket (WS)

A picture is worth a thousand words, and Fig. 9, depicting the side-by-side image of a hypertext transfer protocol (HTTP) request versus a websocket one, says it better than words.[11] On the left is an HTTP request, on the right, a websocket request. It's a direct connection between the client and server.

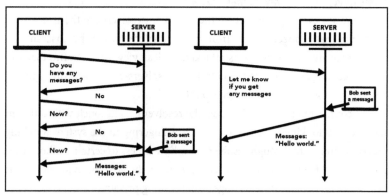

Fig. 9 How HTTP works (left) and how websockets work (right).
Souce: https://medium.com/@td0m/what-are-web-sockets-what-about-rest-apis-b9c15fd72aac.

IP addresses are discovered through WS if the WS server is the same server hosting the website domain. When a query is made in this instance, all the information contained on a web server becomes discoverable through WS. That includes not only IP addresses but nameservers and secure sockets layer (SSL) certificates, as well.

Server-Side Request Forgery

Most IP discovery attacks find ways to intercept or interrupt the connection from user to URL, but a server-side request forgery (SSRF) goes right to the heart of the process and attempts to ascertain IP addresses through the server. This is an example of how minor changes in server configurations can create niche spaces for hacking. Here the goal is to get inside the server to change URL addresses, access server configuration data, and/or forge a connection to internal databases and services. The server on its end (server-side) then attempts to read and input the forged data.[12]

The Impact on Internet Infrastructure

All DNS attacks, all IP discovery methods, rely on specific weaknesses in the Internet's infrastructure. Broken down to the essence of their roles, it's easier to see where the vulnerable spots are along the DNS path and the impact on infrastructure. Netmeister.org illustrates this using Halloween characters,[13] but in what follows, we'll stick to the word scramble and tree analogies to identify the five areas of impact on the infrastructure of the Internet.

Nameservers and Resolvers Make Queries Visible to Bad Actors
Resolvers see every query sent on the Internet. Resolvers are the translators, the things that connect the line from the scrambled word to the unscrambled word. Accessing resolvers gives attackers a clear view of IP traffic that can be intercepted and collected. Centralized resolvers make targeting specific websites and servers easier and cheaper to pull off.

Of course, once a query is made, the resolver gets in touch with different nameservers looking for answers. Attackers lingering in the system watching and collecting data through resolvers now have access to certain authoritative nameservers. Getting to root servers of TLDs is the goal for many malicious actors and can do far more damage than invading privacy.

Port 53 and TCP Traffic Make Confidential Exchanges Discoverable
Data in transit is most vulnerable. Beyond a query, when an email is sent, files are uploaded, or confidential materials are sent through work VPNs, that data while it's in transit is at its most vulnerable. As we all know by now, TCP requests over the DNS are totally unencrypted, and since Port 53 is the same transport used to both make a query and transmit data, in a compromised system, that data in transit is susceptible to interception, collection, or redirection.

There's one development that could protect these transmissions: user datagram protocol (UDP), which is similar to the DNS and actually preceded it. But just as the HOSTS.TXT file got too big to handle all of the traffic, UDP couldn't manage the load or speed of transmission that TCP does. UDP has a smaller bandwidth and can't correct errors in queries the same way TCP is able to. But because few use UDP anymore, it's very fast. Some administrators and DNS operators prefer to do some of their work over UDP, but it's too vulnerable to the actions of bad actors.

In response, UDP source port randomization was developed. It adds two-step authentication to the UDP transmission protocol so that attackers need a transaction ID to intercept exchanges. As well, hackers have to identify the source port, which is randomized, making it nearly impossible to decipher.

Data Exploitation Is Possible Along the Entire Transmission Pathway

One of the biggest vulnerabilities of the DNS is the ability to manipulate data while in transit. Using any of the tools discussed so far to disrupt the connection between the query, resolvers, and nameservers, data can be changed or altered in some way to cause a lot of damage to individual businesses and the Internet's stability.

Bad Actors Exploit Unverified and Unauthenticated Access to Resolvers and Servers

An unencrypted DNS means there are many points along the way where unverified and unauthenticated data can disrupt servers and resolvers while also granting access to legitimate servers and resolvers. DNS hijackers are able to access so much information by securing SSL certificates that they're able to exploit that authority to create phony servers, domains, and IP addresses since resolvers and servers are unable to verify or authenticate legitimate data from fraudulent data.

DNSpionage Agents Are Attacking Nation-States

When 50 different Middle Eastern countries and companies were hit by DNS hijackers in 2018, the IP address for a domain in the Netherlands was seized and used as their main DNS server, directing the compromised infrastructure from the Middle East to there. These hijackers scooped up data in the email exchanges for the government of the United Arab Emirates after hijacking email records contained within that country's DNS servers. With this information in hand, DNS criminals were able to secure SSL certificates for the hijacked domains over the span of hours and weeks.

It's believed these hijackings were the prelude for the ensuing DNS attacks on Netnod and PCH. Basically, DNS hijackers exploiting TLDs were able over time to worm their way to one of the 13 root nameservers controlled by

Netnod while also hijacking domains and servers for entire governments. It appears that getting to those root servers was the goal of these hacks, but a lot of damage could have been done along the way.

These attacks came from unknown hacker rings assaulting government systems. Hostile incursions have also been conducted by countries attacking the Internet infrastructure of other nations. Worst-case scenarios for an all-out cyberwar between nation-states pouncing on DNS infrastructure could leave the entire Internet broken, perhaps irrevocably.

Is the Burden on Corporations Misplaced?

The chief of security for ICANN noted that "many of the best practices that can make it more difficult for attackers to hijack a target's domains or DNS infrastructure have been known for more than a decade."[14] Yet, as I pointed out in the previous chapter, businesses have been slow to realize just how dangerous and threatening DNS-based attacks are. Additionally, as new technologies come online and private corporations implement them, they are unwittingly creating even more opportunities for bad actors to infiltrate their systems, discover IP addresses, or take over their servers.

The survey from the Ponemon Institute shows there was a huge lack of oversight and real monitoring of the DNS threat. Rhino Security Labs notes that a lot of businesses it deals with don't even bother to keep a record of traffic hitting its DNS servers or watching to see if there have been any changes made to any of its records.[15] Organizations that rely on a third party to help monitor their DNS are still vulnerable, since third-party surveillance isn't always 24/7, often only observing DNS activity at different time intervals.

When PCH was hit, its president pointed out that the company uses three individual DNS monitoring services to make sure it knows the moment anything untoward is happening to its servers. None of those services was able to catch the DNS attack on PCH, leaving many to wonder what corporations can do. More to the point, is the burden too heavily placed on corporations?

Clearly, big business is a huge target for DNS attackers. For money or to politically or anarchically disrupt a certain business or government entity, everyone operating online is vulnerable to these DNS security challenges. Corporations, however, have a vested interest in seeing this problem fixed despite evidence showing that, as a whole, they're not treating this threat with the urgency it deserves. To be fair, though, neither are policymakers. That all has to change to prevent a cataclysmic attack on the Internet.

PART THREE

SOLUTIONS

ENCRYPTED **DNS?**

7

Controversy Around Encrypted DNS

Later, I saw that there was a push for "the cloud" to take over yet another part of our Internet. Encrypted DNS is great, we should all do far more of that. But I was (and am) tremendously unhappy that more and more of DNS is now set to move to (among others) Google and Cloudflare control — both of whom protest that they have nothing but the best intentions. But still I see yet more of the Internet getting centralised, and I worry where that will go.

— BERT HUBERT, *POWERDNS TECHNICAL BLOG*[1]

Keeping the Internet free and open has been the guiding principle since it left the realm of military communications to become what it is today. To keep the Internet that way will take effort from all parties involved. Trying to combat the threat of DNS attacks has created controversy around the means to accomplish it. Tech giants such as Google, Cloudflare, and even Mozilla are devising ways to secure their part of the DNS security gap. But in doing so, we're starting to see competing and sometimes conflicting interests emerge that could hinder any progress toward a solid solution to this challenge.[2]

Part of the problem is that while the threat is urgent none of the solutions are by themselves a slam dunk. In fact, if Google has its own encryption software for its browsers but Firefox browsers respond to something different, how free and open will the Internet be? If Google takes the lead, the company stands the best chance of setting the standard. Mozilla came out first with DNS encryption software, and like Google, has gone all-in on one promising solution.

Yet the problem is bigger than a few companies controlling browsers for Internet users, while at the same time, the fact that those companies control browsers — the first step in the DNS chain — means their buy-in is crucial to setting standards. Business has had to take the lead so far, but a coordinated effort between business, government, private citizens, and Internet authorities is the best path forward to a solution that works for everybody.

Take the Internet Engineering Task Force (IETF).[3] This community of Internet engineers comes from a variety of disciplines and backgrounds that contribute to the group's mission. Included are researchers, Internet operators, and network designers all focused on the goal of maintaining the stability of the Internet. Any solution should include folks like those at IETF who have been at this for decades now. Any solution must also be as transparent as the searchable request for comment (RFC) database maintained by PowerDNS where you can view the 297 RFCs related to the DNS.[4] Without this type of transparent and open partnership, any solution to the DNS threat is bound to fall short and continue to create controversy. So let's examine the controversy over the tools to combat DNS attacks.

Encrypting Connections to DNS Servers

Figuring out what section of the DNS to encrypt is the first part of the challenge. In our analogy, it's like trying to decide whether or not to encrypt the lines going to and from the unscrambled words and scrambled words. Should the encryption go deeper into the branches of the trees or the twigs on the branches? Each solution that's been introduced focuses on securing different parts of the DNS, but all of them seem to begin with safeguarding that initial query — the line between the words.

Ideally, that would appear to be the most logical solution. If the query itself is encrypted as it goes back and forth from the user to DNS servers, that would surely limit the opportunities for a rogue third party to squeeze in and intercept the connection. However, that wouldn't prevent everyone from seeing what's being done. Naturally, the ISP that supplies Internet service would still be able to track everywhere a user went online, and we've already discussed CPE attacks that target ISP servers. It would function much like hypertext transfer protocol secure (HTTPS) where traffic to particular websites is encrypted but not every website is secured by SSL certification (some sites are still just HTTP).

Perhaps employing the same type of technology as VPNs could work. VPNs protect users' connections to and from servers from being intercepted once they've been logged into. Simply typing in the address to get to a VPN, however, still makes a connection vulnerable to DNS assaults. Plus, users might attempt to perform queries that leave their local DNS servers in search of proxy servers, resulting in "DNS leaks" that can be exploited.

Obviously, none of these ideas has won the day. What is achieving success is encrypting DNS protocols themselves as well as doing the same with DNS servers and the traffic going to and from them while also dictating what proxy servers to use and ensuring they, too, are encrypted. To date, there are three leading candidates being discussed and in some cases implemented: DNS over TLS (DoT), DNS over HTTPS (DoH), and DNSCrypt. While Cisco is a major Internet security player that does support DNSCrypt, DoH and DoT are clearly in the lead as the go-to solutions right now. I'll delve into those specific DNS solutions as well as Domain Name System Security Extensions (DNSSECs) over the next two chapters, but for now, it's important to understand how DNSCrypt works, since the other two chief solutions were built off that initial encryption technology.

DNSCrypt — The First Encrypted DNS

DNSCrypt first emerged in 2008 in response to DNS spoofing. As with the Internet, its mission changed over time. It went from simply protecting servers against spoofing to becoming a standard privacy tool. To date, it's the first technology for encrypting the DNS and protects more servers through encryption now than any other technology. Over the years, DNSCrypt became the primary solution for people in the know who were concerned about ISP and corporate website data collection and wanted a way to avoid it. DNSCrypt created a version that less savvy users could easily install for Windows. It was also the first to produce DNS encryption for Apple's iOS mobile devices.

For the most part, DNSCrypt is used to block adult content, but Cisco designed its own encrypted DNS based on DNSCrypt technology to prevent access to malicious websites. However, there are limitations to DNSCrypt that take it out of the running as a solution. For one, it's not really transparent. The RFC database is a means for Internet technology solutions to be reviewed and tested, allowing for comments from anyone before implementation. DNSCrypt doesn't have that. It also doesn't provide uniform adoption and implementation, which hinders a universal solution. The IETF supports the leading two solutions — DoH and DoT — over DNSCrypt, backing that counts very heavily in the tech community. Because of that, Cisco and DNSCrypt have adjusted their technologies to include DoH.

ISPs Must Get on Board with DNS Encryption

At the beginning of this chapter, I shared a quote from a forum by a user who expressed concern about Google and Cloudflare shoring up more of their huge slices of the Internet. Beyond the general wariness of the public to the idea of more corporate control over the Internet, users really don't trust corporations or ISPs. Everyone knows that websites that are visited collect data, and so do ISPs. Websites are notorious for targeting ads at their users based on browsing history. Many people just accept this, but a growing number resent the invasion of privacy.

Encrypted DNS will limit the ability of ISPs to track every move online. It clouds their view of user data while leaving enough information for the approved use of traffic tracking, i.e., customer protection. The fact that tech companies are rushing to get to the forefront of a solution to the DNS threat isn't really surprising, particularly for ISPs. Many of these corporate interests benefit from a lack of encryption.

While users distrust those entities with their personal information, ISPs do monitor traffic for security purposes, as well. Having insight into the traffic flowing to and from ISP servers can alert them to attacks or malware infections. However, they also check traffic for copyright infringement, in some places to censor content, and generally to eavesdrop on their customers for their own purposes. As long as customers are limited to the servers of their ISPs, there's no way to avoid being perused and having data collected, but if a DoH or DoT solution can completely bypass ISP servers, this kind of scrutiny could be prevented.

Already there are ways to circumvent local servers by employing open DNS servers conceived by Google and the Asia Pacific Network Information Centre. Cloudflare has also adopted APNIC's open 1.1.1.1 DNS protocol as well as its own open DNS service. All three of these open DNS services are encrypted. The obvious result is that ISPs will be blocked as well as malicious third parties, but that also means these open DNS servers will then have a full view of user traffic. All parties have pinkie-promised not to do any monitoring other than for malicious traffic, but there's no guarantee of that.

Google Faces Congressional Antitrust Backlash

The beginning of December 2020 was the first time in decades that an anti-trust lawsuit was brought before the U.S. Congress. Facebook was in the hot seat for buying What'sApp and Instagram. A year prior to that Google faced questions from Congress when the tech giant revealed its intention to encrypt DNS for its users. Google's plans to implement DoH for its websites raised concerns with the congressional committee overseeing antitrust laws.

Congress sent a letter asking Google if implementing DoH on browsers used by billions of users around the world would prevent advertisers and ISPs from gaining access to the data collected from those users through Google's website.[5] In response, ISPs argued with Congress that the change had the potential to "foreclose competition in advertising and other industries."[6] Since 2016, when net neutrality rules were all but obliterated, ISPs have had a freer hand to use data collection for targeted advertising based on user behavior, a lucrative business for advertisers and ISPs but a clear intrusion on user privacy.

Google, along with Mozilla, a company that also plans to roll out DoH, rebutted those concerns by reassuring Congress that this change is only an effort to prevent unauthorized access to user traffic. The president of Mozilla also pointed out that ISPs were fighting this necessary fundamental change in DNS security purely for economic gain from access to user data. The goal of DoH implementation isn't to prevent data collection by advertisers and ISPs, but perhaps it's a happy benefit for users.

Mozilla worked fast to institute DoH during the summer of 2020. Google chose specific DNS providers to test the technology before implementing it for all of the company's users. Regardless of congressional concerns or the discontent of ISPs with the move to encrypted DNS, the fact of the matter is that DNS encryption is going to happen. Without this change in the fundamental security of the DNS, the Internet will remain fundamentally insecure and vulnerable to catastrophic attacks.

Tech Experts Differ on New DNS Standards but Agree New Ones Are Necessary

Over these first seven chapters, I believe it's clear there needs to be a standard use of encrypted DNS moving forward. Most if not all tech experts agree, as do many major Internet security providers. The problem is to find a consensus on which standards to adopt. I believe that considering the concerns of all sides will help elucidate a robust solution. Let's start with the biggest worry of all parties involved: centralization.

Despite Google's protests that it only has the best intentions implementing DoH, the reality is that it's a huge company with a gigantic market share. Any plan for encryption by Google will affect billions of users and thousands of competitors and vendors and would thus divert enormous amounts of traffic to its network of servers. Just the idea of Google attempting to redirect its browser users to its own DNS encrypted servers worries practically all the parties involved. The company has responded to this concern, saying in a statement to *Ars Technica*: "Google has no plans to centralize or change people's DNS providers to Google by default.... Any claim that we are trying to become the centralized encrypted DNS provider is inaccurate."[7]

Local DNS controlled by state and municipal governments could help prevent this kind of centralization, but we'll get deeper into that in Chapter 11. Right now, this solution isn't even on the table but is a way to overcome the first and fundamental concern with DNS encryption through DoH. Besides this issue, other concerns really break down into which side of the equation people are on. Let's take the user end first.

Users have as equal a stake in ensuring the DNS is secure as any other operator in this space. It's user data and the traffic over the DNS that bad actors threaten. Such concerns can't be overlooked or downplayed, particularly in the interest of profits. For most users, any discussion of the DNS or DNS security might as well be in Greek. Therefore, it's incumbent upon those involved to figure out the solution that considers the user end in everything.

This is especially necessary when contemplating that most attempts to either protect or collect data happen in the background and that most users are completely unaware of what's going on. ISPs generally control resolver settings for their DNS servers, while their customers usually have no idea what that is or how to change it to give themselves more control over what happens to data.

Browser providers such as Mozilla and Google are incredibly important stakeholders in securing the DNS and have a lot of common interests with their users. At the same time, Google, Cloudflare, and Mozilla compete with one another for more user traffic. Their approaches to DNS encryption implementation differ, too. Mozilla chose Cloudflare as the administrator of its recursive resolver, while Google picked Chrome. Whichever one is first with the most widely accepted solution will garner so much new traffic that it's also likely to draw more scrutiny from Congress and more attention from DNS attackers.

It's the balancing of their self-interest to achieve financial success with the safety and security of their users that makes these voices so important in any discussion of DNS encryption standards, but they shouldn't have the only or even the greatest influence. Truthfully, Mozilla has a far smaller market share than Google, but its history has proven to be user-focused. In that respect, it's incurred less skepticism from its users.

Instead of slowly moving toward DoH adoption like Google, Mozilla has jumped all-in, moving all of its users over time to DoH and blocking access to its browsers from websites that aren't encrypted. Google, on the other hand, will revert to unencrypted DNS if it detects a query for a website that's not enabled with DoH. We'll soon know how well either of these implementations go over, but protecting browsers alone won't solve the DNS security problem. On top of that, without a standard for DNS encryption, there will be gaps in DNS security — the very thing everyone is trying to prevent.

CYBERDEFENSE

8

Controversy Around Encrypted DNS — DNSSEC

The general public is only recently hearing about the DNS, but behind the scenes IT security professionals have been developing technologies to protect it for years. Several industry players adopted DNS encryption tools more than a decade ago and have been using technology like DNSCrypt and DNSSEC for a long time. In 2020, Cloudflare announced that it would be instituting DNSSEC as part of its plans to combat DNS attacks.[1]

So why are neither DNSCrypt nor DNSSEC a serious part of the discussion as a solution to secure the DNS? The answer is worth understanding. Think about it. DNSCrypt was introduced more than a decade ago. DNSSEC preceded DNSCrypt by three years. And yet we're still trying to solve the same problem. Clearly, neither of these technologies has been able to prevent attacks on the DNS. From the beginning, there were shortcomings with both of these technologies, but the idea that something is better than nothing led to some early adoption.

Both of the leading solutions being championed today similarly have shortcomings but are improvements on DNSSEC and DNSCrypt. There are businesses and proponents of each technology pushing adoption now, despite knowing that each still falls short of a singular solution to the DNS threat. The goal of this book is to prevent a solution that ultimately leads us right back to where we are now — still trying to figure out the best way to prevent attacks on the DNS. With DNS assaults growing more lethal and severe every day, we can't waste another decade on partial solutions. So let's look at the pros and cons of DNSSEC and what it might still have to offer as a solution to this urgent problem.

The "Kaminsky Attack" and the "Fundamental Flaw"

In cybersecurity circles, everyone knows what the "Kaminsky Attack" is, but generally speaking, most people have never heard of it. Named for Dan

Kaminsky, an Internet security expert and a member of the United States Computer Emergency Readiness Team (US-CERT) program, the Kaminsky Attack happened in the summer of 2008 when Dan Kaminsky conducted a strike on the DNS, revealing to the world for the first time its fundamental security flaw.[2] He showed that the algorithms used to create unique IDs for data in transit were limited to just 65,536 possibilities and that with the right tools they could be easily guessed in seconds by hackers.

Kaminsky figured this out in an effort to fix this flaw. He was designing a patch, but the attack design leaked before he could release it, and the rest is history. Copycats jumped on the attack design and have been reworking it ever since to make these attacks more and more sophisticated. Sadly, with this knowledge in hand, many website administrators chose to leave it alone for the most part, fearing that servers wouldn't be able to verify thousands of transaction IDs per second without slowing the Internet down considerably while also creating instability. The solution was to reduce the TTL frequency to limit the amount of time a hacker would have to try to guess the transaction ID.

Since that discovery, the types of attacks on DNS servers that were predicted have come to pass and then some. It was foreseen that spoofing would be far too easy to do and enable cache poisoning to run rampant. DNS hijackings were forecasted, as well as redirections, interceptions, bypasses of authentication measures, and more. Kaminsky, and others like him working in cybersecurity today, are raising those same alarms and working toward a comprehensive solution to this extremely complex and serious challenge.

One of the major weaknesses of the DNS is in the resolution process. It's not just that it's unencrypted; it's that there is no way to authenticate data, which is where DNS attacks are seizing control of SSL certificates and gaining the authority to make changes. What DNSSEC does is provide authentication through electronic signatures attached to the data going from the unscrambled word to the scrambled word. Each step along the way is protected by a verifying signature so that data can't be hijacked or spoofed.

In 1993, years before Kaminsky's attack, the IETF began trying to figure out how to protect data in transit over the DNS.[3] It wasn't until 2005 that DNSSEC was publicized by the IETF as the best method to protect the DNS. Yet, to this day, it isn't standard. Fifteen years after it was first declared the answer to the DNS security threat, it still hadn't become universally accepted, despite the fact that DNSSEC does get to a very critical component of the DNS security gap.

The main reason why DNSSEC has lacked popular support is that it has a glaring weakness. Even after adding layers of randomization, diversified portals, and more ID requirements, the DNS remains vulnerable to attack, though the additional layers of protection have made decryption of authoritative signatures much more difficult.

Solving the DNS Authentication Problem

DNSSEC tries to solve the authentication problem in a way the two leading technologies being discussed to combat the DNS threat don't. Instead of focusing on securing the browsers or the individual puzzle sheets, DNSSEC protects the line in the middle and the process for figuring out where to direct the line correctly. It shields the resolver by adding a layer of authentication to data while they're in transit. Currently, the resolver doesn't have the ability to discern between good and bad when it comes to data. DNSSEC adds a signature that tells the resolver and the server that this is good data.

Think of digitally signed documents. There's a unique identifier that's recognized by courts when a document has been signed electronically, not in person and in ink. Digitally signed documents with unique IDs confer the understanding that no one has changed the document and that it's authentic. Digital signatures do the same thing through DNSSEC.

The nonprofit Internet Systems Consortium (ISC) announced its support for DNSSEC in 2020, just as Cloudflare did. For those using UDP ports, the ISC advocated expanding them. It also recommended that anyone employing recursive nameservers with caching, including ISPs, should implement DNSSEC.[4] The ISC doesn't claim that DNSSEC is the ultimate solution for securing the DNS as a whole, though, but it does argue that DNSSEC is the ultimate solution to prevent DNS spoofing.

The Role of Recursive Resolvers in DNSSEC

Resolvers notoriously will return the first answer they get from a nameserver whenever they receive a query, as long as it appears to match the question. It's like a bouncer at an 18-and-over nightclub where minors know they can get in without an ID. A lot of underage drinkers are going to show up trying to get in. In the same way, hackers take advantage of the openness of recursive resolvers. Nick Sullivan, in his article for the *Cloudflare Blog*, laid out a DNS attack on a root server this way:

- Pick a domain whose DNS entries you want to hijack.

- Send a request to the recursive resolver for the record you want to poison.

- Send many fake UDP responses pretending to be the authoritative server with the answer of your choosing (i.e., point the record to an IP you control).

- If the fake response gets there first, the recursive resolver believes it at face value, returning it as a legitimate response to the query. It then caches that response until the TTL expires.[5]

Now all the hacker has to do is send a request for the fake address that's been implanted in that cache, and *boom*, a cache-poisoning DNS attack. For anyone looking for that domain, the recursive resolver will now return the malicious website instead of the legitimate one. Realistically, though, most people don't have the expertise to pull off a hack like that. In reality, it's not as simple as it appears. Hackers still need algorithms that can guess the ID in time, the request has to be aimed at the correct nameserver, and it has to target the precise UDP port. But for the most dangerous hackers today, an attack such as this one is mere child's play.

Protecting DNS Records Through DNSSEC

An essential term highlighted in "Essential Terms We Need to Know" at the end of this book is *resource records*. In the tree analogy, resource records are the branch and all the leaves and twigs on that branch. To return a positive query, DNSSEC requires the root server to have a key that matches the key attached to the resource record, which adds another layer of depth to secure the resolution process. These keys are maintained by IANA, one of the organizations that manages the 13 root servers and provides authority over domain naming.

Adding this layer of authentication enables resolvers to return a definitive response when the record doesn't exist. Instead of merely passing it along, DNSSEC encryption gives the resolver more authority to verify record requests, and without the key, it returns the request as "nonexistent." These new record types have been added to root servers, along with several new kinds that have been added over the years.

Why Not DNSSEC?

While there's nothing technically wrong with DNSSEC, it can't be the end-to-end solution needed to close the DNS security gap. It has its pluses, combating the problem at the root-server and resolver level, which is critical. But it doesn't have the support of most domain administrators, and even with security improvements, it's still unable to completely close the chasm.

DNSSEC is compatible with both encrypted and unencrypted resolvers, but therein lies another fundamental flaw. As long as a query stays on a DNSSEC-encrypted pathway, there's no problem. But the second the query leaves that "chain of trust," a vector opens for a DNS attack.[6]

9

Controversy Around Encrypted DNS — DoT and DoH

People of goodwill can reasonably disagree on a solution to the DNS security challenge while agreeing on the end goal. Those with an opinion about DoT versus DoH are passionate about their belief that one or the other is the right solution. Some cynically dismiss each solution, while others have a vested interest in one solution over the other. It's going to take people without a dog in the race to figure out the answer. People like me in cybersecurity are for the most part solely focused on getting the solution right to prevent the worst-case scenarios that keep us up at night.

The IETF has given its blessing to both DoH and DoT as a means to secure the DNS between recursive resolvers and servers. Although both use encryption and authentication to secure data in transit, a query isn't prevented from leaving a DNS server, thereby posing the risk of exposure to threats lingering outside the chain of trust within encrypted pathways.

Despite this knowledge, Mozilla began work to figure out how to implement DoH for all of its browser users in 2017. In 2020, it started making DoH encryption the default for its browsers.[1] This effort isn't so much a way to secure the DNS overall but is aimed primarily at assuring its users that its data is more private and less susceptible to snoopers and data collection when using Firefox.

While there are definite shortfalls with both DoH and DoT, it's surely an improvement over what we have now with totally unencrypted DNS. Both DoT and DoH encrypt data in transit over TCP instead of UDP so that nameservers don't just accept the first answer to queries they receive. Both encrypt lookups or queries, though both leave the solution to the vulnerability of proxy servers unanswered.[2]

There are pluses and minuses for both DoT and DoH. With some leading tech giants already diving in head first with one solution over the other, it's necessary to examine them both objectively to decide which one makes the most sense.

Pros for DNS over TLS (DoT)

Writers at Infoblox drew a good comparison for the difference between DoH and DoT.[3] They compared it to the contrast between VHS and Betamax, home video systems that came out about the same time. Betamax never took off the way VHS did. As the Infoblox piece points out, it's not as if VHS was so much better than Betamax. In fact, one could argue that the quality of video on Betamax was better.

The real big distinctions were in cost (VHS was cheaper) and the ability to record longer videos on VHS than Betamax. Similarly, DoT and DoH are very alike and are basically trying to fix the same problem but with slightly different methods. Let's examine the pros that have been established with DNS over TLS (DoT).

No one is arguing that DoT is the end-to-end solution we've been dreaming of — not its creators or its proponents. What proponents do argue is that it does a better job of encrypting data in transit than DNSCrypt, DoH, and DNSSEC. Instead of simply sending traffic (on compatible browsers) along encrypted pathways that can be tampered with, DoT bubble-wraps data that's then sent along the DNS over TLS.

What that means is that data is secured on a deeper level within the roots of the Internet tree as opposed to the superficial puzzle-sheet level. None of the data moving over DoT travels across the more open and lesser-used UDP and instead journeys solely along TCP/IP traffic.[4] It also improves upon a component of DNSSEC that's worth keeping, which is the extra layer of authentication. DoT employs a public key based on the simple public key infrastructure (SPKI) guidelines in which a unique key is given to the certificate holder of a particular IP address.

Already many public Wi-Fi providers offer DoT using public servers that rely on public resolvers to handle queries. Android and iOS mobile operators also depend heavily on DoT to secure traffic. Mobile use of DoT is on the rise.[5] Like VHS, one of its top features is that it's pretty simple to implement for network administrators, making it the more cost-efficient option.

By encrypting at the root level or the transport layer, DoT is able to adapt to multiple-class types beyond HTTP (i.e., DVR and mobile devices in addition to Internet browsers). DoH focuses largely on protecting browser traffic, which has its own flaws. DoT is considered to be more secure because it does more than protect browser traffic. Both encryption tools slow processes a bit (we're talking milliseconds here), but DoT is a bit faster.

Cons for DoT

At first glance, it may appear as if DoT has so many pros that the cons couldn't possibly outweigh them. However, let's take a look at them, because they're important cons. A glaring flaw is the potential for DoT requests to be blocked.[6] To avoid UDP ports, DoT requests go over a frequency, if you will, that doesn't come in clearly and gets marked as suspicious by firewalls.

The burden of certification and verification on servers using TCP also hinders performance under DoT. Another big question with DoT is in the problem that it solves — authentication. While DoT does verify the authenticity of resolvers and servers, the packets of data containing the resource records (RRs) themselves haven't been verified. They've been bubble-wrapped, yes, but what is inside the bubble wrap and has it been tampered with? DoT can't answer that query.

Finally, DoT comes up short in the same way that DoH does. It focuses solely on browser-level authentication. DNSSEC protects records, resolvers, and servers; DoT safeguards traffic to and from servers at the HTTP (browser) level. Neither is singularly the solution, but combining the two doesn't exactly fix the problem, either.

Pros for DNS over HTTPS (DoH)

Among the major Internet companies offering DoH are Google, Apple, and Microsoft — almost guaranteeing that it becomes standard.[7] Frankly, to the broader public, implementation might seem sudden, but the truth is, Google and Mozilla have been planning on introducing DoH to their users for the past few years. In essence, DoH encrypts the line between the words. When a query is begun using a Firefox browser, the query is encrypted as it searches for a resolver to direct it to the correct server.

Speaking of resolvers, DoH employs a specific list of recursive resolvers called trusted recursive resolvers (TRRs). Agencies enrolled in this program agree to implement certain protective standards that guard against user data collection and sharing in order to be included in the list of resolvers deemed safe by DoH-encrypted browsers. DoH encryption also keeps third parties from intercepting data by dictating which resolvers to use.

Some of the major proponents of DoH are end users and groups calling for more privacy online. People who spend a lot of time going from browser to browser tend to prefer DoH over DoT.[8] In that regard, it makes sense that the most popular web browsers are leading the way to standardized adoption of an encryption tool that protects browser data.

Web companies have powerful opponents in ISPs, though. By switching browser users to DoH, many of the local servers provided by ISPs will be bypassed in favor of public DNS servers, greatly limiting the ability of ISPs to collect customer data.[9] Internet providers are working a two-prong strategy: petition to limit Google's (and thereby Microsoft's and Mozilla's) ability to override its control over user queries or adopt some version of DoH, as well.

User privacy is the big winner when it comes to DoH. It is less about securing the backbone of the DNS as it is about protecting user data from spying in order to win more traffic. It's working, too. Users who are tech-savvy enough to understand how to reconfigure browser privacy settings see this move as taking the power over private data out of the hands of ISPs and putting it in the control of users.

Cons for DoH

If DoH becomes the default standard as Mozilla is implementing now, most users are likely to keep it as a default without realizing they're bypassing their local ISP servers. Parental controls and some firewall protection provided by ISPs might be rendered powerless if local servers are bypassed in favor of trusted public servers directed by a particular web browser's DoH protocols. To keep everything transparent, Mozilla issued an open comments period in November 2020 to help improve the rollout of DoH.[10]

So while DoH does provide users the opportunity to exert more control over their data privacy, it's more than likely that the bulk of users will never access their default settings. Another downside is that it doesn't operate at the system level where apps and mail servers are located. As it's currently designed, DoH is only able to encrypt traffic at the browser level. In fact, DoH is listed in the RFC database as a web application security solution. It does nothing to protect data going to unspecified resolvers.

Another area of concern is where DoH protections are aimed. As Netmeister points out, the way DoH is configured, it's designed to distrust the network and default resolver operators. That assumes those operations have been hijacked in some way. After a resolver or network is hijacked, it's too late. DoH provides protection for the web applications using DoH in the browser but leaves all other web traffic vulnerable. So a hijacked resolver will still result in compromised systems as vulnerabilities in other web traffic continue to be exploited.

Part of the controversy over DoH lies in who ultimately controls the resolvers charged with securing IP traffic. Nearly all home-based users operate under the resolvers of their ISPs. DoH, through a web-based application, does take that process out of the hands of snooping ISPs but then gives it to corporate partners of Google or Mozilla. As long as they keep their word that they won't do the type of data collection that unnerves users so much about their ISPs, it would be a plus for users, a con for ISPs.

And yet network providers will still have eyes on user traffic; they just won't be able to collect the data. Not to mention that there are a number of protections that users will lose if they bypass their ISPs. For instance, most ISPs provide firewall protection, content filtering, malware protections, and more. Those all disappear once a public resolver is chosen, or Mozilla opts for the user.

One huge concern for network administrators is figuring out whether or not DoH over TCP traffic will be as flexible as UDP has been for scaling up as the Internet has expanded. With some providers going to DoT and others choosing DoH, it might add more complexity to an already tough problem. In a confusing and complicated system, attack vectors tend to open up in places no one suspects. Just the fact that implementation makes it necessary for administrators to operate a separate resolver to work with other systems causes adoption to be difficult. Adoption will require bigger libraries, data packets, and more coding. Moreover, latency is higher for DoH than for DoT.

Two last things. DoH does authenticate resolvers but can't vouch for the resource records — just like DNSSEC and DoT. Regardless of the solution, that dilemma still remains. And finally, something that's creating consternation for all parties involved is the idea of centralization. Switching to DoH and moving management of Internet traffic to public resolvers will centralize DNS control among browser providers and public cloud providers in a way that could limit the openness of the Internet.

Comparing DoT and DoH

"The reality is that DNS over HTTPS and DNS over TLS are slightly different standards for implementing the same DNS protections," writes Mike Schroll, co-founder of DNSFilter.[11] Side by side, there really isn't much difference between DoT and DoH. They both attempt to solve the same problem:

encrypting traffic over the Internet. However, there are some important differences. There's an argument that can be made that DoH is too far removed from the root layer, making it less viable than DoT, which operates just one level above the Internet. This allows DoT adoption for IoT devices and mobile devices, as well as for web-based applications, whereas DoH is strictly for web-based applications.

For data protection, both tools prevent man-in-the-middle attacks caused by spoofing legitimate websites. Both also thwart data collection and monetizing by ISPs and third-party snoops. A true side-by-side comparison from NETSCOUT surveyed DoT requests versus DoH ones for a month. DoT servers were accessed seven times more frequently than DoH, and two companies benefited the most from that traffic — Google and Cloudflare.[12]

Keep in mind that Cloudflare is now Mozilla's default recursive resolver. Traffic over Cloudflare could be users accessing Firefox browsers that are encrypted through DoH. Google employs six different resolvers, including Cloudflare.[13] For its part, Mozilla has gone much further than any other browser provider in declaring pro-user protections — vowing to shorten TTLs to one day, a pledge never to share data with a third party, and delivering maximum transparency to its users to prove that its data hasn't been stored or collected.

Fears of Centralization for Both DoT and DoH

"I would love it if there were 100 other encrypted DNS providers that customers could choose from…. We think that would be great. I get that there being a limited set of choices doesn't feel good. But there's nothing proprietary about this. You can download open source software and run this today," says Matthew Prince, the CEO of Cloudflare.[14]

Cloudflare's CEO makes a really strong point. At the same time, everyone agrees that centralization for any entity online is a bad idea. There are groups integral to the operation of the Internet jumping in to try to combat this drive toward centralization for both DoH and DoT. If either were an end-to-end solution, there would probably be far less reticence about a centralized solution. Nonetheless, considering the downsides to each technology, and as different powerful actors in the equation choose sides, the Electronic Frontier Foundation (EFF), a privacy advocacy group, is encouraging ISPs to compete rather than complain.

The EFF argues that if ISPs encrypt their DNS servers, they could act as TRRs. Of course, users would expect the same kinds of privacy pledges and assurances they've received from Mozilla and Google from their ISPs. If ISPs became part of the solution to encrypt the DNS, it could help prevent the type of centralization everyone fears. It's one solution, but not likely to see mass adoption by corporations earning lots of money selling the user data they collect.

Already U.S.-based firms such as Mozilla have had their plans rejected by the United Kingdom. When Mozilla announced it would roll out DoH as the default for all its users, the United Kingdom revolted. In response, Mozilla assured Britain that it wouldn't implement a similar default DoH plan in that country to the one it planned for the United States.[15] Mozilla hasn't given up yet, though. The company is in search of a European partner to help encrypt more DNS data over its browsers.

Considering Mobile Device DNS Encryption

Much of the discussion around DoT versus DoH has centered on web-based applications. Yet today the vast majority of Internet users access it from a mobile device. With the likes of Google, Microsoft, and Mozilla adopting different forms of web-based encryption, it's worth considering the DNS variety for mobile devices.

In 2020, Apple announced plans to follow suit with the major web browser providers and offer DNS encryption. How it intends to implement that might provide clues to solving the problem overall. Apple's Mac operating systems and its iOS will offer both DoT and DoH.[16] Network administrators and app creators have several options for executing DNS encryption for Apple apps They could opt to make the singular DNS encryption server through Apple the default server to be used for all its apps. If instead the company wants to point its users to an encrypted public server, it will offer a network extension app that can be configured.

There's also a method for configuring DNS encryption settings through device management. Users will be able to "opt in" when Apple asks if they'd like to make Apple's encrypted server the default, or users could go in and specify which server they'd prefer to have for their apps. Apple goes even further by enabling its DNS encryption service to detect VPNs or other server settings provided by a customer's ISP (like parental controls) and will alert users to give them an option to permit content their ISPs might block. Existing apps could be easily updated to include DoH and DoT traffic.

Unlike Apple, Android will continue to operate standard DNS but will upgrade to DoT whenever it's detected. Since Google owns Android, it, too, uses DoH encryption, but at the root, not just at the browser level. Microsoft also plans to allow DoH in its operating system while maintaining DoT as its default DNS encryption tool.

Limitations of Both DoT and DoH as a Standard Solution

Without doubt, there are limitations that prevent either DoT or DoH from being an end-to-end solution to the DNS threat. With all the effort to enable encrypted web browsing through DoH and DoT, neither solves the fundamental flaw in the overall security of the DNS. I'm talking about the authorities. Of all of these encryption tools from DNSCrypt to DoH, none of them answers the plain text problem for requests going to root servers on the DNS. None of the above encrypts those unencrypted plain text messages.

Part of the problem is that the lead advocates for DoH and DoT are invested parties. These measures help to secure their mobile device operating systems or their web browser security, but those are just a small part of the problem. They're superficial fixes that don't get to the heart of the challenge. Moreover, tech companies are in competition with one another. Google wants people to use Chrome, and Apple desires people to employ Mac.

When someone using a Google browser wants to access Windows, what happens when one browser supports DoH and the other only backs DoT? Without standards or regulation, there will always be some shortsightedness built into any solution to the DNS problem.

SOLUTIONS

10

Solution — Diversify DNS Servers

Now that I've laid out the different security solutions being debated, which one should the world adopt? All of the above are correct! For people who are singularly focused on securing the spine of the Internet without a vested interest in either technology, the answer is diversify, diversify, diversify. There's a place for each of these technologies as well as others in the effort to secure the backbone of the Internet.

Why hasn't the problem been fixed after all this time? Experts in the field realized two things when Kaminsky's attack was revealed over a decade ago:

- "The vulnerability itself has not been fully fixed, as it is a design flaw in DNS itself."[1]

- "The problem in general terms is described as insufficient randomness."[2]

In 2018, the ISC conducted a survey to measure the interest level of its business clients in implementing DoH and DoT. What it found was that three-quarters of those who responded were against applying DNS security solutions that increased privacy for their users. Less than a third were interested in adopting encrypted DNS.[3] Regardless, DoH is moving forward in the browser sphere, while DoT is quickly becoming the default for mobile devices. Free public servers are also leaning toward DoH.

When everything is factored in, including how the DNS is designed at its root, how vulnerable the DNS is, and the different technologies meant to solve the problem, there's far more to Internet security than privacy and data collection. However, a similar survey of the general public would probably yield even bigger numbers of users completely disinterested in protecting the DNS.

The difficulty here is public awareness. When the people who have worked on the problem for decades still can't achieve consensus, it's no wonder the public isn't part of the debate. The only thing that everyday users know for sure is that having their data collected for advertising purposes behind their backs is bad. Too many have no idea how deep the predicament goes, and the same can be said for corporations. This book, and many of the articles cited in it, are written by people sounding the alarm so that once and for all everyone can put their minds together to close the DNS security gap.

Features That Should Be Included in an End-to-End Solution

Data centers around the globe swaddle their servers in layers and layers of encryption and firewalls. Most browser companies and anyone operating a business online go the extra mile to prevent hacks like the ones we've seen in the past. But we're seeing attacks far beyond anything known previously. And yet it's the root of the Internet where that thin layer of unencrypted data resolution happens that makes the Internet so vulnerable, and worse, no one so far has come up with a solution to fix it.

There has to be a comprehensive solution that provides encryption at every level while maintaining the free and open nature of the Internet. It's a tall task, but people have already been piecing it together for years. There are things we know that have to be accounted for when devising a definitive resolution, one that's proactive, nimble, tracked, coordinated, and distributed across multiple servers, tools, and providers.

Unfortunately, everyone has been working in separate silos: browser operators looking to secure their specific data traffic, and big business aiming to prevent large hacks that lose customers and exfiltrate business data. The time has come for all these entities to come together to create an end-to-end answer combining many different methods.

If we combine some of the tools already out there, an end-to-end solution starts to come into sharper focus. Viewing it through that lens, there are at least six specific features that any end-to-end key to secure the DNS must have.

Server Flipping

Starting from the premise that online attacks and failures are going to happen, EasyDNS began working on a DNS solution it calls proactive nameservers (PNs).[4] Being the victim of "blow-ups" in the past, the company realized that the only way to prevent an entire network from going down during an attack was to have one, if not many, backups.

When there's a hint of trouble in the system, PNs automatically flip to an identical server on the network. They provide multiple fail-stop servers to pick up overflow traffic coming from a downed server. Users on the other end barely notice anything is even wrong. They're able to continue operating online as if nothing happened. Meanwhile, a worming attack that might have spread like wildfire was stopped in its tracks when the first server went down.

PNs work because all the trusted nameservers within the "backup" pool are constantly synced together in real time. These servers cover the same zone as the downed server so that users are rolled over to another nameserver automatically. There's no downtime and the intrusion can't continue to spread and infect other servers.

Even if the system reacts to something that isn't actually an intrusion, the system slows only slightly and very temporarily before returning to normal. This idea of networking servers in a safe zone with this type of rollover technology is essential for any diversified solution to DNS security.

Diversified DNS Servers

Once again, the folks at EasyDNS are way ahead of the game when it comes to out-of-the-box solutions to DNS security. In addition to server flipping, its servers are diversified. There are certain nameservers within each data zone, but the company also coordinates with outside servers that have been verified and are updated in real time with the PN master file.

The idea here is that if a network of servers is hosted by the same provider and the provider is attacked, all the servers will go down. But if a diverse group of providers — at least two or three additional providers outside a given network — the network can be triple-protected from collapsing.

These external white-listed nameserver IP addresses are allowed to mirror the PN so that the fail-safe rollover is diversified, just in case of a future attack where all the protected network servers are infected. There's a backup to the backup located inside a network-approved and verified safe zone. EasyDNS allows its clients to configure its nameservers in a variety of ways.

A unique feature of PNs is that instead of keeping all servers active at all times, backup servers hum along passively until they're called into action when there's a downturn. One benefit is that it keeps the backup servers to the backup servers twice removed from an attack so that action can be taken to protect the real-time master file maintained by passive servers.

Organizations that don't have the resources of a major retailer to pool and operate a bunch of nameservers on their own could partner with a similar organization and build a protective alliance within their server networks using the EasyDNS model.[5] All partners within the group could maintain master files for servers within the same network community utilizing a specified selection of trusted providers as their fail-safes.

Localized Outages Using DNS Anycast Protocols

Think of DNS Anycast as water used to dilute a glass of alcohol or a very strong cleanser. Instead of employing a group of servers in a protected network, DNS Anycast utilizes points of presence (PoPs) distribution to diversify data traffic. PoPs are basically relay servers spread around the world.[6] They help move traffic going to a website in a particular geographic location and keep it from getting jammed in transit, diversifying the pathways that data have to travel to arrive at a specific IP address.

While DNS Anycast can't stop DDoS attacks aimed at creating bottlenecks in Internet traffic, it helps to diffuse traffic so that servers aren't overwhelmed to the point of crashing. PoPs localize traffic so that IP traffic coming from Australia to access an American website doesn't have to travel all the way to the United States to log into an IP address through a server geographically located in America. Instead, PoPs relay the request through different points that go to the website without having to access the server of origin.

Again, this technology is clear-eyed about the fact that DDoS attacks are going to happen, so the goal is to nullify them. What DNS Anycast does is help stop an assault from spreading globally by localizing traffic. Instead of a server that's under attack being downed by millions of requests multiplying globally, DNS Anycast "will act as a 'sinkhole' for the attack traffic — pulling it away from your other global PoPs."[7] Adding this feature to an end-to-end solution helps mitigate global DNS hacks by preventing them from proliferating.

Real-Time Updates for TLDs

Generally speaking, top level domain or TLD zones are updated in real time, but not all of them. For backup servers to work, updates across the network have to happen in real time at all times. Some domain administrators set a time for their updates every hour or even every day. There are too many seconds in a day to allow gaps in updates if we're going to close the security gaps in the DNS infrastructure.

Isolated and Encrypted Nameservers

Encrypting nameservers is only half the battle. The other things that have to accompany any DNS security strategy are isolation and separation. First, nameservers should never be grouped together with other components of a network infrastructure. For instance, databases shouldn't be maintained and accessible along the same network pathways as nameservers.

The goal is to separate each part of a DNS infrastructure while also maintaining synchronization. As long as everything is synchronized, if one part of the infrastructure goes down, say, mail servers, network traffic can still hum along because they're walled off in different silos. Remember, when there's any sign of trouble that might cause mail servers to go down, the infected traffic won't be able to continue traveling along a continuous network of servers if passive servers are employed to step in to ensure mail servers don't fail.

To sum up, the writers at EasyDNS say it best:

- Treat every DNS component, be it a vendor, data centre or cloud provider, as a discrete, logical unit

- Stack up multiple "units" that are separate from each other

- Keep them configured, ready and hopefully in-sync with your current zone data

- Have the ability to activate them when the S hits the F, or else, just run them all, all the time.[8]

Secured Data Trail Left by DNS Queries

Every query and every result leaves a trail. We all know that websites collect user data; some even announce they're collecting little bits of data in cookies. Most systems record parts of each query, while some record all of it and log this DNS activity. Imagine if a hacker could get into the cache of a server storing all the data left along the data trail by billions of users worldwide. It could be a huge gateway into a catastrophic attack on the DNS.

Focusing on securing the data as it comes and goes is crucial, but any solution to solve the DNS puzzle must include securing the data trail left behind. The trail of data left by queries always leads back to a server somewhere. Protecting that server and defending the data in transit is imperative. Making sure to erase the footsteps left in the dirt along that trail is also critically important.

The Magic Bullet

Surprise — there is no magic bullet. Or better yet, another way to think of it is that maybe we need more bullets. The fact of the matter is, the best Internet security experts today can't predict what's coming down the pike. We can imagine and prepare for the worst-case scenarios and anything in between, but the effort to find the silver bullet is perhaps part of the reason we're still searching for a solution.

The answer can't be a few giants in the tech industry attempting to secure their little pieces of the trail, leaving the rest of the path wide open. The magic bullet lies within all these solutions and with every party involved in solving the crisis. The solution is bigger than corporations or one single government because the problem is that big. Now that the challenge has been identified, the goal is to put the world's brightest brains together in a race to secure the DNS the way the scientific world discovered vaccines to combat COVID-19.

PART FOUR

CONCLUSION

DEFENSE

INTERNET
AS A PUBLIC UTILITY
IS FAR OVERDUE

11

The Argument for Control of Local DNS Servers by Government

We're looking at something that has truly become a necessity for survival. It's critical to the functioning of society. Treating the internet like electricity or water is the way we need to think about it.

— LISA GILBERT, EXECUTIVE VICE PRESIDENT, PUBLIC CITIZEN[1]

Reading the title of this chapter, I wouldn't be surprised if at least a few readers rolled their eyes at the thought of government controlling something like DNS servers and doing it well. It's been conventional wisdom for an entire generation or more that government is the problem, not the solution, that private corporations are better at handling the big things. Conventional wisdom it might be, but it's verifiably not true.

For the really big things, we depend on government. Look no further than the U.S. military, spy technology, managing utilities, and in the past, building transcontinental railroads, canals, and interstate highways. And don't forget, it was the U.S. government that invented the very idea of an Internet! When it comes to controlling threats as deep and serious as those marshaled against the underpinnings of the entire Internet, only government can organize a solution this big. But the truth is, government can't do it alone.

Securing the DNS is going to take a comprehensive answer that pulls together knowledge and expertise from government, the private sector, citizen activists, tech experts, and global partners. What we already know is that it can be done. We've accomplished big things like this before. Electricity began as a private good that only the wealthy could afford to experiment with, but electrical fires and the impracticality of a private corporation funding streetlights demanded that the government step in to provide electricity as a public good while supplying the means to fund and regulate it.

The telephone was once the new age technology of the day before it evolved into an essential good that necessitated the creation of the infrastructure to deliver that service to the public. It was a public/private partnership that required government regulation, and yet that didn't stop private phone companies from becoming extremely profitable, even to this day.

Everyone uses the Internet for one thing or another — email, audio and video calling, online banking and learning, cloud-based applications, remote work, and even checking in with our doctors. With so many people depending on the Internet for basic needs, how can we be sure this infrastructure will maintain its quality against ever-increasing demand? Similarly, considering that the Internet is a source for accessing education, employment, and health care, we're forced to regard it as an *essential* commodity for sustaining modern human life.

As it stands now, the Internet in the United States is a messy collection of different elements: "small pipes to homes, broadband service, cheap Wi-Fi routers with limited ranges, big pipes to companies,"[2] as well as countless devices requiring repair and security updates. All in all, we have the classic specimen of a multi-point failure scenario.

Despite the risk of DNS-related attacks constantly looming over our heads, we can mitigate or eliminate a considerable number of existing assaults using a well-organized DNS infrastructure. That would not only restrict access to servers to those who legitimately need it but also help ensure the integrity of data users according to their designated roles.[3]

But the big elephant in the room, besides the political and economic will to confront the problem, is the type of infrastructure investments needed for there to be government control of local DNS servers. This type of nationwide infrastructure will cost hundreds of billions of dollars, requiring legislation on Capitol Hill, along with enough legislators with the determination to pass it.

Consider the fact that America watched in horror in 2007 on a sunny August day in Minnesota when the I-35 bridge collapsed with heavy midday traffic stuck on it. More than a dozen people lost their lives. After investigations into the collapse were made, a design flaw was discovered that contributed to it. More importantly, the bridge was nearly 70 years old and hadn't been inspected or upgraded to handle decades of increased traffic weight, which was one of the factors that led to the weakening of its overall structure.

Four years after the disaster and two years into President Barack Obama's administration, calls for a 21st-century infrastructure bill were put forward as the solution to decades of neglect for all U.S. roads and bridges.[4] In 2014,

Obama proposed a funding package of just over $300 billion that was meant to update and repair every deficient road and bridge in the country.[5] That bill never passed. In November 2021, however, the U.S. House of Representatives passed President Joe Biden's $1.2 trillion infrastructure bill, which the president signed into law. The bill includes $65 billion for broadband, with $42 billion to be administered for grants to states by the National Telecommunications and Information Administration.

America's Crumbling Digital Infrastructure

Any architecture for local DNS servers controlled by government will be built on top of the existing infrastructure. The I-35 bridge collapse exemplified the overall state of the country's existing physical infrastructure. But before I get into the nation's crumbling digital infrastructure, it's worth looking a little further into our deteriorating general infrastructure.

In the aftermath of the Minnesota bridge collapse, investigations were done and commissions were formed to ascertain how it happened and what was needed to fix things. What was discovered by the American Society of Civil Engineers (ASCE) is that America's entire essential infrastructure is just as bad. In 2013, the ASCE gave the United States a "D+" overall for our infrastructure. And yet nothing has been done in the near decade since to improve the situation while our infrastructure has only aged and fallen into further disrepair.

Fig. 10 The aftermath of the I-35 bridge collapse outside Minneapolis in Minnesota in August 2007.

Source: https://en.wikipedia.org/wiki/I-35W_Mississippi_River_bridge.

Most alarming, the report found that it's specifically the nation's "critical" infrastructure that's in need of most repair and that everything is at a critical breaking point. Similarly to DNS servers, it's quite possible that our essential infrastructure can no longer meet the demands of the country today. Schools are deficient, public transit is subpar, our systems for supplying electricity, energy, water, and yes, roads and bridges are all crumbling or are in a sorry state. Distressingly, DNS and wireless technology didn't even make it onto the list of inadequate infrastructure.

After the report, in an effort to get Republican votes for an infrastructure bill, the Obama administration traveled to then Speaker of the House John Boehner's district to highlight a near-half-century-old bridge — a main artery between Ohio and Kentucky — that was on the verge of collapse. The appropriations subcommittee examined the report detailing the problems with our "obsolete" roads and bridges.[6] But again, nothing was done. Over the four years of President Donald Trump's administration that followed, there were repeated plans for an "infrastructure week" that never materialized. To date, we're still living with the same physical infrastructure judged obsolete several years ago while grappling with the need to update and repair an area of our infrastructure that's been wholly overlooked.

The ASCE took a look at America's digital infrastructure in 2011 and gave it the same grade as our traditional critical infrastructure — D+.[7] For one thing, as the ASCE points out, the Internet's demand is far greater than what it was ever designed to supply. On top of that, there's no coordinating organization for America's digital infrastructure. Depending on where one lives, there might only be limited dial-up. Other places might have Wi-Fi, but it might be too patchy to be of use because there are no towers or servers in range.

Since the Internet is now essential to daily life, not just in the United States but around the world, it can no longer be thought of as an amenity or a luxury. By all accounts, it's a necessity. There's no private business willing to, or rationally would, take on the responsibility of making sure there's reliable, first-rate broadband and Wi-Fi access even in the remotest parts of the United States. Therefore, it's the U.S. government, as with all public goods and utilities, that will have to take on that burden. However, the same problem that still confronts our critical physical infrastructure more than a decade after the I-35 bridge collapse is the same one that confronts our digital infrastructure — lack of government funding and real infrastructure investment.

Local DNS Requires Real Infrastructure Investment

As I was formulating the argument for government to take control of local DNS servers to provide Internet for all while simultaneously securing the DNS, I thought about comparable infrastructure challenges in the United States that were overcome in the past. Again, the interstate highway system came to mind. I wondered how much it had cost to build upon the Lincoln Highway, the first transcontinental road that preceded it. Why did President Dwight Eisenhower decide in the 1950s to create interstate highways and why was it considered important for the defense of the country?

As a U.S. Army colonel in 1919, Eisenhower took a road trip with a convoy of military vehicles that was the first of its kind to drive from coast-to-coast across the United States. The journey from Washington, D.C., to San Francisco took more than two months, and the future president wrote that the miserable state of the Lincoln Highway could present a national security risk. Troop movements, he warned, would be arduous and inefficient across muddy, broken, washed-out, and crumbling roads and bridges. What if, he posited, the United States was invaded? Then, after serving as Supreme Allied Commander in Europe in the Second World War and being thoroughly impressed with Germany's autobahn highways, Eisenhower, as president, enacted the National Interstate and Defense Highways Act in 1956.[8]

More than 60 years have passed since that law was signed. With a price tag of $250 billion in today's currency, the bill created 41,000 miles of new highways across the country and from north to south. Although it was projected to take a decade to complete, the project wasn't finished in reality until 2018 when the last part of the I-95 corridor was finally completed. To be fair, I-95 is the biggest chunk of the 41,000 miles of interstate highways, spanning almost 2,000 miles and handling 40 percent of the GDP that flows through the United States. That strip alone cost $425 million and took 60 years to complete. Frankly, we don't have that kind of time to shore up our digital infrastructure's security vulnerabilities.

Anyone who has ever driven on the interstate highways will probably admit that Eisenhower made a good investment providing this valuable service to the public. What took two months to travel before the interstate highway system in 1919 can now be driven from New York City all the way to Los Angeles in fewer than 27 hours. Even with the hottest, biggest SUV, can you imagine road travel in America without the interstate system today?

That's how we have to start thinking about our digital infrastructure and Internet services. Just as with our roads and bridges before the interstate highways, our digital weaknesses are a threat to national security. It's going to require a nationwide investment similar to the interstate highway system, but instead of taking decades upon decades to build, we have to develop it quickly. Moreover, we have to be prepared to continually update these systems. Unlike roads and bridges, it doesn't take half a century for digital technology to become obsolete and fall into disrepair. Think about it: our digital infrastructure itself is only a few decades old and a lot of it's already obsolete and substandard.

First-generation home computers were built on the back of the telephone lines that had previously been laid when that technology was new. Computers required dial-up modems to connect to the Internet using a phone line. Cable companies created even faster Internet connections that didn't require dial-up modems but instead relied on broadband cables. Today, we're using fiber-optic cables and wireless signals from servers and towers. Yet there are at least 24 million Americans who haven't seen any upgrade in their local digital infrastructure since the dial-up modem. They're still waiting on broadband to get to them.[9] It's worth reiterating that the Internet is now essential.

Estimates put the price tag for providing universal access to broadband in the United States at $100 billion. But to provide local DNS servers, we have to think bigger. Should a combination of broadband, fiber optic, and towers be employed, or should government back one technology over the other? All of the equipment that goes into shoring up the digital infrastructure costs money, managing it is going to cost money, and staying on top of security updates and infrastructure updates are going to be crucial.

New departments will have to be established to handle the different aspects of the nationwide architecture of local DNS servers working in concert with local and state digital infrastructure departments. There has to be a national standard for what counts as reliable Internet service. The program would have to start with the most acute areas where there's little to no Internet service. Already states have designated areas as underserved based on the speed of their Internet services. The $100 billion price tag would provide 100 megabits per second (Mbps) at a time when some states don't classify areas where Internet speeds are as low as 25 Mbps as underserved areas.

Making the Case for Congressional Funding of Local DNS

Looking back at the interstate highway project for guidance on congressional funding, it might surprise Americans today to know that the federal government footed 90 percent of the bill.[10] States pitched in the last 10 percent, and repair and maintenance from that point on was to be funded by a gas tax. The gas tax, which hasn't been increased since 1993 and isn't tied to inflation, was set between 18.4 and 24.4 cents per gallon.

Considering how much the cost of everything has risen since the 1950s, it's no wonder our critical infrastructure is in disrepair if we've only been spending a quarter per gallon of gas for care and maintenance. To put that in perspective, taxing regular fuel at 18.4 cents per gallon when gas in 2020 averaged around $2.35 per gallon means that only about an eighth of the cost of a gallon of gas went into the coffers for highway upkeep.

States can't cover the deficit, and thus, we end up with a bridge collapse in Minnesota during rush hour. As for the 60-plus-year I-95 project, it's expected to be bombarded with an increase of traffic topping 85 percent by 2035. Meanwhile, the ASCE has projected that spending on critical infrastructure over the next five years will fall a full $2 trillion short of the necessary investments essential to handle these increases.

Paying for government control of local DNS doesn't have to be painful. Just like the phone companies of the 20th century, there will be plenty of opportunities for private corporations to formulate profitable public/private partnerships to provide Internet as a utility. Initial funding will require some state, federal, and municipal bonds; grants will have to be available to states with rural areas the farthest behind in digital infrastructure; and the federal government could provide loans to states and businesses to incentivize digital infrastructure investment.

Currently, ISPs are able to set prices, determine where to expand service, and decide what counts as quality Internet speeds.[11] That kind of corporate control of a crucial commodity has left an estimated 90 million Americans in areas where Internet service is deemed "suboptimal." Attempts to expand that reach so far have been meager at best. In 2018, the Trump administration proposed $1.35 billion in grants and loans to invest in broadband construction and upgrades in rural areas — not nearly enough to take care of adding broadband service alone.

All the more reason to aim for a coordinated, comprehensive, government-backed and funded solution to this problem: an answer that accounts for the mistakes of the past — like a gas tax that never increases — and lays down real investment dollars from the start with a world-class Internet system that will prevent the need for trillions of dollars of massive upgrades down the road. Just like DNS security itself, diversity is the answer for funding the new highway project — the 21st-Century Information Highway Revamp Project, if you will.

Americans Are Cheating Themselves

Equitable distribution of funds for this endeavor will require congressional oversight to determine what areas are and aren't "underserved." As I noted earlier, the standards for low versus reliable Internet service have to be decided — which areas should receive the largest investment up front? The Federal Communications Commission (FCC) sets the standards for which areas are underserved, and yet states have largely left it up to ISPs to ascertain if an area has sufficient Internet access.

Keep in mind that if funding is based on whether an area is served or underserved, there could still be many pockets of the population missed within highly serviced areas. These are all funding questions that must be hashed out so that the new digital infrastructure that requires constant vigilance from new and evolving threats never falls into obsolescence or disrepair. Seven years ago the ASCE estimated that by 2020, U.S. infrastructure would need investment upward of $3.6 trillion to accommodate increasing demand. There had been no new infrastructure investment since 2009 when $31 billion was added to the American Recovery and Reinvestment Act after the economic collapse in 2008 until November 2021 when President Joe Biden signed a $1.2-trillion, five-year infrastructure bill into law.[12]

Making an appeal to the public for infrastructure spending is usually easier to do when it's framed as new jobs — which it is. Just as the interstate highway project created tens of thousands of new jobs from coast-to-coast, so would a new digital infrastructure bill. However, Americans are still greatly opposed to any tax increases as Gallup noted in a 2013 poll that found "two-thirds of Americans would oppose a gas tax hike of up to 20 cents a gallon, even if the money were to go to improving roads and bridges and building more mass transit."[13]

Maybe another way to come at this for the public is to point out that Americans are by and large being cheated. Since 2010, access to the Internet has increased by nearly 20 percent while the average price for service — around

$60 per month — has remained relatively the same. However, when costs and services Americans are getting are compared with those for users everywhere else in the world, Americans are getting a "lousy deal."[14]

In fact, compared to 206 other countries, the United States ranks 119th, showing that we're among the seven countries paying the most money for Internet service. When it comes to access to high-speed Internet, Romania even beats the United States. As Ernesto Falcon, a senior counsel for the Electronic Frontier Foundation, puts it, "Americans have the slowest, most expensive internet in the world."[15] He didn't mean it literally, but he's close.

Tens of Millions of Americans Left Behind

Susan Aaronson, the director of the Digital Trade and Data Governance Hub at George Washington University, has said that Internet access "is essential to equality of opportunity, access to credit, access to other public goods, access to education."[16] One reason that an estimated 25 million, and by some estimates more than 150 million Americans, have no Internet access is because of "relatively stable pricing." To average income households, $60 per month for Internet service doesn't seem so bad. But for households making less than $30,000 per year, $60 per month ends up being too high a price for close to 45 percent, according to Pew Research.[17] Nearly half of households making less than $30,000 per year don't even own a computer, let alone have Internet access.

Pew's research also found that 1 in 10 Americans don't have or don't use the Internet, while Microsoft points out that of those with broadband access to the Internet, a full 162 million are hampered by suboptimal Internet speeds — nearly half of the total population of the United States.[18] Without dedicated policy-making, the lack of high-speed broadband can affect the lives of a considerable portion of the population. If the federal government provides $100 billion worth of investment to enhance the national broadband capabilities to 100 Mbps, it can easily create a reliable publicly owned broadband network.

In the end, treating the Internet as a public utility can help policymakers to transform the lives of millions of Americans. By making Internet service a public utility, we can create a win-win-win situation. First, it would expand access to the Internet to all Americans no matter where they live. It would help secure the DNS through very localized DNS servers, it would have the added benefit of improving our national infrastructure both digital and physical, and it would be a massive jobs program.

When thought about like that, it begs the question: "Why haven't we made the Internet a public utility yet?" Considering a service as an essential public utility boils down to how critical an impact it has on the lives of its users. With the onslaught of COVID-19, it has become clear that the Internet can give both people and businesses tremendous earning potential and enhance their quality of living. Without it, "you'd be in some form of quarantine unable to access information, with far fewer distractions and means to connect with others, and no way to work (if indeed your job has moved online in these difficult times). And if you were an indigent parent, you wouldn't be able to maintain some semblance of continuing education for your children."[19]

Having access to fast and reliable Internet means that people can continue with their education, access remote health care, earn a living remotely, and maintain social, personal, and professional relationships even as they're immobilized in their homes. The question that hasn't been asked that needs to be posed is: "Is Internet access a right or a privilege?" We've been debating that same query over health care for three-quarters of a century. However, the urgency of the situation requires that we answer it yesterday, and we all have to agree that it has become a necessity for the pursuit of life, liberty, and happiness — hence, a right.

No "Free-Market" Cure for Public Internet Access

From the beginning of the COVID-19 pandemic, many corporations, including ISPs, have tried to make life easier for people to access Internet services. Zoom expanded free teleconferencing for remote work, and cable and mobile providers provided a couple of months of free Internet and phone services to many of their customers. However, everyone knew these weren't sustainable solutions to the problem. Eventually, companies had to begin charging for their services despite the pandemic in the United States exploding to catastrophic levels.

The already buckling weight of demand on the Internet has only compounded since the pandemic started. As with heavy traffic on roads and bridges, over time, that weight is going to cause a break. It's happening already as video-conferencing experiences drops, freezes, and delays. Doctors' visits are being canceled or postponed because of problems with telemedical equipment. Yet without ISPs and telecom companies supplying their services, life as we know it would come to a screeching halt.

At the same time, neither users nor the government can rely on the kindness of corporations to make Internet access reliable and universal. There's no free-market solution for this quandary. However, the FCC under the Trump administration, headed by Ajit Pai, took the position of corporations, calling the Internet a "free-market service ... not a utility," adding that "the FCC's light-touch approach is working."[20] For at least 90 million Americans, the "light touch" hasn't been effective. Even as a free-market service, the Internet is a "direct descendent" of the phone system in America.

Just as Americans paid for the upkeep of the interstate highway system through a gas tax, once phone companies fell under the oversight of the FCC, the Universal Service Fund (USF) was created to pay for access to telecommunications services. Established in 1997 after the Telecommunications Act of 1996 was signed into law, the USF was tasked with increasing the range of telecom services across all U.S. states and territories. The annual budget of the USF is between $5 and $8 billion, but ISPs have extraordinary control over where those funds are directed — not the FCC.

Take for instance the USF budget for 2019. In it, low-income areas received only 13 percent of the $8.4 billion allotted. Rural health care only got 8 percent of the money, while high-cost areas shared the bulk of it at 60 percent — more than even schools and libraries.[21] Despite being able to direct where taxpayer dollars for telecommunications should go, ISPs aren't required to contribute to the USF, even though those dollars help to increase their revenues and customer bases. Unlike the gas tax, the amount of money Americans put into the USF has doubled in the face of falling taxable revenues.

Deregulation of the telecom industry hasn't only cost Americans more money for dwindling services, it's squashed competition, aggregating into a few powerful companies.[22] In addition to congressional concerns for potential monopolies among social media companies and DNS encryption for browser owners, decisions around costs and funding for Internet access that so many Americans depend must be a top priority, as well.

Internet as a Public Utility Is Far Overdue

Los Angeles Times columnist David Lazarus writes: "After months of being stuck at home, many Americans know full well that there are three things they can't live without. Two of them are power and water. The third, I'm sure, will be obvious to all. Internet access."[23]

The Internet as a public utility is an idea that's far overdue, since we're well into the Internet Age and still leaving many people behind. The first COVID-19 case was reported in the United States in January 2020, and since then, Americans have added greatly to the enormous increase in Internet usage. But the pandemic is global. To say that Internet use increased by 70 percent in 2020 only captures the extent of this sudden rise in demand when we remember that people around the planet are staying at home.

Of course, statistics-wise, Americans have been hit the hardest by the pandemic. The United States by far exceeded the rest of the world in the number of COVID-19 cases (tens of millions) as well as the number of deaths (hundreds of thousands). While other countries were able to resume some degree of normal life in many ways after months of fighting the virus, the United States was in much worse shape and far from normal even after more than a year and a half into the pandemic. Therefore, the need to really deal with the DNS threat urgently became all the more acute.

On top of the vast disparities revealed by COVID-19, the necessity to distance has resulted in an extraordinary economic downturn. As services continue to fray while the Internet remains overtaxed and overburdened, everyday life for many Americans with limited access to the Internet gets increasingly more difficult to manage. As Catherine Powell, a law professor at Fordham University, says, "If it wasn't clear before, it's now crystal clear that internet access is necessary to survive in our contemporary world, similar to electricity."[24]

CORPORATIONS

12

The Role for Corporations

Generally speaking, U.S. corporations have maintained a largely adversarial relationship with governments ever since the 1929 stock market collapse that led to the Great Depression in the 1930s. Before then, corporations often called on governments to use the National Guard and local police forces to squash worker strikes — something that would be completely illegal and unheard of today. Yet when it comes to our cybersecurity posture, this combative relationship has only made us more vulnerable. Top that with the fact that corporations aren't so antagonistic when they need the U.S. government's help in the face of nation-state hacks and a growing number of DNS attacks.

As a business owner myself, I know that businesses are motivated primarily by earnings. True, companies might provide services or products they believe in, but corporations and the boards that govern them were created to make profits. Profits are at the center of many of the DNS's vulnerabilities that I've discussed in previous chapters. Consider the fact that private corporations have largely been allowed to dictate the coverage map for Internet access in America, leaving an estimated 162 million Americans without essential high-speed Internet.

Cue December 17, 2020, when the US-CERT team announced to the world that the United States was the unwitting victim of an ongoing DNS attack that hit "many Fortune 500 firms and a broad swath of the federal government."[1] Responsibility for the attack was, not surprisingly, attributed to Russian hackers who managed to infiltrate SolarWinds' software update management system. As far back as September 2019, hackers began implanting attack code in the Orion threat monitoring software without being noticed.[2]

For more than a year, hackers operated unabated before the breach was discovered on December 17, 2020. It broke records as the most massive attack on some of America's most sensitive national security agencies. Included in the assault against the U.S. government were:

- The U.S. Department of Energy.

- The U.S. Treasury Department Systems.

- The U.S. Justice Department.

- The U.S. Commerce Department.

- The Federal Courts Administrative Offices.

- And at least one U.S. senator.

Microsoft, along with other investigators, identified dozens of targets of the attack, all of them considered high value. Some of what was taken was extremely sensitive encryption tools maintained by some of our top national security agencies, leading to more concern among IT experts about future DNS attacks involving credentials and authoritative servers. Some experts even advised burning the whole thing "down to the ground"[3] to completely eradicate the hackers from U.S. agency and corporate networks. At the very least, experts will have to spend months chasing the data trails possibly left behind by the hackers.

In the meantime, it hasn't escaped the attention of gigantic tech companies that they, too, were victims of this attack, with Microsoft admitting a few days after the alert was issued that the hackers had accessed its "internal source code."[4] At first, it appeared that dozens of companies were hit. By the first week of 2021, 250 corporations and organizations were known to have been breached by this attack. A week later, it was clear the hack was ongoing and growing exponentially. There were more than a thousand known victims of this assault by the end of January 2021, with cybercriminals specifically targeting cybersecurity firms, including the widely used FireEye and hundreds of "industrial organizations."[5]

Called a supply chain attack, this kind of hack features cybercriminals who find a vulnerable company, in this case SolarWinds, that "supplies" software to many other systems. By infiltrating SolarWinds and infecting its product, downstream customers were breached just by automatically updating their SolarWinds-provided software.

Can you imagine what would happen if this supply chain attack breached Windows' automatic updates? Every computer would automatically download and install infected software during the next update cycle. Every computer would have a potential asset for the perpetration of new attacks like spying or network-flooding DDoS assaults.

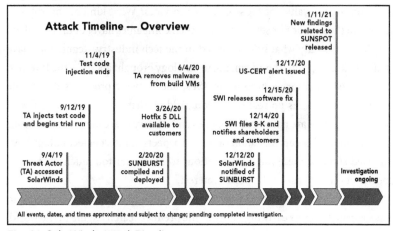

Fig. 11 SolarWinds Attack Timeline.

Source: https://orangematter.solarwinds.com/2021/01/11/new-findings-from-our-investigation-of-sunburst.

A supply chain attack can be perpetrated through DNS strikes, as well. What if hackers changed the Windows update Internet address to point to their own compromised systems? Every user whose computer engaged Microsoft's security suite would visit the faulty address and unwittingly download exploited software updates, running silently in the background, as would every other system that looked up the changed DNS address.

To put it bluntly, there's no way an individual corporation or even a band of corporations could handle a threat of this size alone. This is the point where adversarial corporations tend to put down their cudgels, hoping the U.S. government can save them. A schism between corporate America and government leaves both sides blind and does nothing to prevent future attacks that cause even more damage. The word going forward in cybersecurity has got to be *cooperation.*

The Dangers of Tech Companies as Natural Monopolies

Imagine a service, product, or tool that everyone needs. When someone figures out how to monetize such an innovation, the potential to sell billions exists, and that entrepreneur becomes the sole proprietor of a specific good and could make a fortune. In the same way, the largest tech companies in the world have been able to amass hundreds of billions of dollars over the years — largely due to the novelty and complexity of regulating the Internet combined with the power naturally pertaining to them for inventing or creating goods or services everyone wants. How much control would such companies have over setting the value for those goods or services? What kind of control over access to those goods or services would such companies have? Sound familiar?

This is exactly what has happened in the tech industry. Regulations have failed to keep up with the advancing technology brought about by the Internet. Social media platforms, web hosts, ISPs, and browser providers dictate the rules because there's no real regulation. Add all that to the fact that a few of these companies are natural monopolies and it's easy to see how lax regulations and the inevitable centralization of certain aspects of Internet technology have allowed some of these huge corporations to accrue far too much unchecked power at the expense of the public interest.

To be clear, it's totally within Google's rights in a capitalist economy to take advantage of its early ingenuity as the premier search engine in the world. There are others in the same field, but none compete on a global scale the way Google does. The same can be said about Amazon — technically other companies can compete, but they're greatly outmatched. It's the very nature of capitalism to take a useful idea and turn it into profits. Herein lies the conflict when it comes to the role of corporations in securing the DNS. If there's a company out there that could come up with *the* single solution to the DNS problem, it would be the next natural monopoly.

Part of the reason why browser providers such as Mozilla try to get out in front on DNS encryption is to secure their positions in the market as indispensable entities. Here's another thought experiment: what if the Internet itself wasn't a government-conceived project but rather something invented by one person? That person would be more powerful than Facebook's inventor and founder, Mark Zuckerberg, a college kid who had no idea what a little campus rating system would turn into, or how much power it would give him.

When corporations get that big, for the public good, they must eventually be regulated when they become essential. It's clear that the Internet is an essential good. However, the way it's regulated now, it's as if Thomas Edison created the only company that could provide electricity, and to this day, the "Edison" company was able to dictate who in the United States was able to access electricity, could set the prices at whatever the market would bear, and could stomp out any competition. Just think how many American households would be without electricity simply because they resided in rural towns with too few people to make investing in expanding access there a good business decision.

Local DNS control that's regulated and deemed essential turns the control of where and how to deploy these crucial goods over to public policymakers.

In an environment where tech behemoths have so much power, it's the smaller players that are granting greater control to users locally. As the ISC puts it, "Enterprise networks and service provider access networks are actually becoming natural bastions of local control, slowing the inexorable increase of centralization on the Internet."[6] Arguing against widespread deployment of DoH, the ISC warned:

> While there may be some efficiencies and optimizations possible with greater centralization, history and experience has shown again and again that eventually we will regret relinquishing control to a few unregulated, self-interested giant tech companies. Eventually, this loss of independence and self-determination will lead to less freedom of choice, less competition, and less privacy and security.[7]

From the perspective of corporations, regulating the way data flows over the Internet is hitting them where it hurts. Let's be honest. Corporations depend on that data for multiple reasons. Nearly all businesses monetize data through advertisement dollars. Corporations operating online amass website data to gain insight into their traffic, users, and customers to better tailor their ads and services so they can increase profits.

Trying to keep the quiet part quiet, when telecoms and ISPs brought their complaint about mass adoption of DNS encryption by Google to the U.S. Congress, part of their argument was to say: "Google's support for DNS over HTTPS (DoH) could interfere on a mass scale with critical Internet functions, as well as raise data-competition issues."[8] In other words, who gets to keep making money off data if access to private user data is severed?

The debate is also making strange bedfellows. The same groups arguing for less corporate spying on user activity and collection of user data argue against DoH adoption by the major browser providers. Their fears of too much centralization overrule the need for more encryption. Plus, as I've already laid out, encrypting data flowing over browsers is only one part of a comprehensive DNS security solution. At the same time, there have been hard clashes over the limits of corporate sovereignty versus the government's needs.

I wrote in my book *Security and Privacy in an IT World* about the fight between Apple and the FBI over access to a terrorist's cellphone, which highlighted this conflict.[9] Terrorists had pulled off a mass shooting and attempted bombing in San Bernadino, California, and the feds wanted access to the phone left behind to thwart any other plots and to locate possible co-conspirators.

The issue was taken to the Supreme Court when Apple refused to provide a back door to its encryption codes:

> Critics of DNS over HTTPS do recognize the irony of pushing for less encryption out of a desire to protect people when the security and cryptography communities overall take a hard line against law enforcement on the value of encrypted communication platforms free of backdoors. But the difference, they say, is that end-to-end encryption or encryption at rest cuts everyone out except the data's owners, while DNS encryption only shifts trust.[10]

MAD Between Corporations and Their Customers

Before the collapse of the Soviet Union, the catchphrase of the late 1980s was mutually assured destruction, or MAD. At the time, the United States and the Soviet Union had so many nuclear weapons pointed at each other that if one shot off a nuke, it assured the total destruction of the other. It's what kept the Cold War cold for so long — the idea that a nuclear launch by either side would create a chain reaction that would destroy the world many times over. Today, there's a new sort of MAD. It's mutually assured *digital* destruction. I'm referring to the relationship between corporations operating online and their customers.

Losing customers due to a data breach is just one of the ways business suffers. When Target's stores were hit by hackers in 2013 during Black Friday, it was due to a point-of-sale (POS) attack when someone either internally or externally was able to infect the store systems — which are connected nation-wide — with a virus on a portable device. Both Target's physical stores and its online store suffered the effects.

Customers were reasonably cautious about handing over their credit card information to a company, even one as well known as Target, after hackers accessed millions of customer accounts and the data contained within those records. Compared to its previous sales the year before, Target's profits plummeted by nearly 50 percent after that breach, plus there was a dip in its stock price of 10 percent immediately after the hack. Home Depot's high-profile breach exposed at least 65 million customer records, resulting in a tangible loss of over $60 million.[11]

In January 2010, US-CERT began issuing weekly alerts warning businesses, agencies, and partner nations around the world about the most recent cyber threats. It's a team effort that depends on governments and private businesses around the globe to help thwart massive disruptions of the Internet.[12]

Compared to the types of DNS attacks we're now seeing, those earlier hacks seem tame. We know for certain that the SolarWinds attack was well thought out. It was planned long in advance and lurked in the system for months without detection. What was actually taken in the attack is still unknown. Additionally, "research suggests the insidious methods used by the intruders to subvert the company's software development pipeline could be repurposed against many other major software providers."[13]

Since the disclosure of the SolarWinds hack in December 2020, more and more details have emerged to show just how dangerous that breach was. In addition to the initial software update hack, a third strain was "installed via the backdoored Orion updates on networks that the SolarWinds attackers wanted to plunder more deeply."[14] Evidenced by the increase in DDoS attacks, cybercriminals can also use the DNS as a means to launch devastating cyberattacks on companies. These assaults temporarily wipe out access to websites for millions of users in a single strike.[15]

Even some of the world's leading brands such as Amazon, Reddit, the *New York Times*, and PayPal have succumbed to this threat and had their applications temporarily booted off the grid. That's why the DNS has a foundational role to ensure the operation and security of both external and internal network applications.

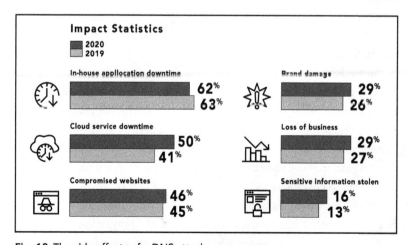

Fig. 12 The side effects of a DNS attack.
Source: www.techrepublic.com/article/how-dns-attacks-threaten-organizations.

Corporations in the financial industry lose the most money with every DNS attack. According to one survey, each time a financial services business is hit, it costs on average $1.3 million.[16] While there are many political reasons that international hackers target a specific type of industry, the majority of bad actors are looking for money as well as disruption. It's social media, ISPs, and the entertainment industry that see the most attacks every year, while schools and research institutions have to worry about exfiltration the most.

As research from the Ponemon Institute that I highlighted in Chapter 5 demonstrates, corporations aren't nearly prepared enough to handle the DNS threat. Awareness of the danger has been growing. Nearly 100 percent of companies surveyed by the International Data Corporation (IDC) in the 2020 Global DNS Threat Report issued by EfficientIP said that DNS security is considered "critical." But only 25 percent go beyond manual tracking to analyze the threat data coming in, while half simply rely on automated monitoring systems. Partnering with the government to help secure the DNS is mutually beneficial for corporations, all of which need updated and universally accepted standard practices for monitoring the DNS risk to everyone.

Local DNS Protects Cloud-Based Services for Corporations

Another aspect of DNS security overlooked by corporations is captured in the aforementioned statistic from the Global DNS Threat Report. Just over half of businesses surveyed rely on security solutions like those offered by FireEye and SolarWinds for their DNS security management. But as we have seen, even those reliable security providers aren't immune to the DNS attacks seen nowadays. Moreover, much of their data and the protection of that data have moved to the cloud.

Instead of having an IT team on-site charged with monitoring and thwarting threats to the corporate network, those duties have largely been handed over to third-party cloud service providers. When there's an assault on the network, corporations have to rely on a third party to assess the attack and to remove the threat quickly. According to the same study, with every hack, the clear majority of corporations experience hours of downtime that hinders their business operations.

Within a properly monitored DNS infrastructure, there's plenty of data to be gleaned from it to increase security. However, it takes expertise and constant vigilance to stay ahead of these evolving threats — the kind of monitoring that can't be solely left up to algorithms and automated systems. In addition, using third-party cloud providers within a digital infrastructure that's unequipped to service local DNS traffic means that businesses are dependent on remote servers and resolvers to handle their traffic. This, too, creates a huge vulnerability for the DNS security of a company's entire digital infrastructure.

Moving to locally based DNS servers controlled by a government agency enables businesses to rely on more secure local DNS servers, thus cutting off one of the biggest gaps in the Internet's overall DNS infrastructure. It's the same reason that businesses often put their main servers closest to headquarters but also maintain shared recursive and authoritative servers with their branch offices in other locations. It helps to keep company data secure within a closed network. But for companies like ISPs and web browser providers, there's no real way to close their networks completely as public providers. And as businesses providing a public good to the public, it makes sense to bring them within the regulation and protection of the U.S. government.

Combating the Hegemony of a Few Selected Providers

If they're being honest, the top CEOs of the major tech companies in the world would admit that the real problem for them in accepting government oversight is that they'll lose control of user data that has turned into a lucrative revenue stream. Cable companies, all of which have been hemorrhaging customers as so many millennials and even younger people ditch cable in favor of streaming over the Internet, are incentivized to try to maintain a grip on reliable revenue streams like money for user data.

Meanwhile, telecoms are charging more and more for Internet services to compensate for that loss.[17] Telecoms and ISPs continue to argue that their price increases are necessary for investment in new high-speed lines. Public advocates argue that this is a lie, that, in fact, there's no real physical investment happening since the fiber-optic cables already in the ground don't need massive amounts of investment and rely mostly on software updates for upgrades. Certainly, they don't require the 10 years of steady price increases that customers have been paying for those "investments." However, as Harold Feld, senior vice president of the advocacy group Public Knowledge, has said, "The only reason for why our broadband prices are relatively stable is because there isn't much competition."[18]

Maintaining their position in their respective slices (and sometimes that of others) of the Internet marketplace is the guiding principle, evidenced by the fact that leading broadband companies have spent millions of dollars fighting federal open Internet regulations.[19] One example of this was seen when the issue of net neutrality came into public light.

When the "net" is neutral, service providers can't slow, block, or prioritize one type of data over another, meaning they can't manipulate service to ensure those who can afford to do so will spend more for better broadband. In 2017, telecoms found a powerful ally in government. The FCC, led by Trump appointee Ajit Pai, formerly a lawyer for Verizon, repealed net neutrality protections after a notice period plagued with allegations of unfairness.[20] Some of the companies supporting the repeal of net neutrality protections appear to have contributed money to campaigns waged by Internet "trolls" that post support for the repeal of net neutrality, which skewed the official record meant to reflect what the public actually wanted — net neutrality.[21]

In 2017 and 2018, Comcast spent more than $30 million lobbying Congress.[22] At that point, even Comcast's shareholders demanded more transparency from the broadband giant after laying down that kind of cash for lobbying against net neutrality. Comcast's concern was primarily that the company's activities would lead to a public backlash and greater demand for municipal broadband, which would inevitably erode the firm's profits.

In essence, the shareholders' position was: "If the public truly understood just how much money Comcast was spending to ensure it controls Internet access, voters would themselves be lobbying politicians for a public option that could ultimately undermine Comcast's ability to attract any customers at all." Since the end of net neutrality in 2017, there have been several challenges to the rules set by the FCC by U.S. state attorneys general as well as by Internet advocacy groups. Yet the federal circuit court ruled against them, deciding instead in favor of allowing telecoms to throttle Internet service in order to charge higher rates for increased speed.

Importantly, the court also held that the U.S. government can't prohibit states or other localities from creating public options. Perhaps boldness, perhaps desperation, but these pro-corporate moves at the expense of the public good might have gone too far. In upholding local government's right to provide a public option for Internet access, the court took the FCC to task for disregarding its duty to consider how its decision threatens public safety, lifeline service, and broadband infrastructure. Not only had the broadband providers proven that they don't feel responsible to the people they serve but they also gave mayors and governors good reason and plenty of motivation to act boldly on behalf of their constituents.[23]

Most users pay for DNS service administered through their ISPs when they sign up for cable despite ISPs being perhaps the worst kind of DNS provider any customer could have. An ISP might intercept DNS queries and provide its own responses to direct a browser to anything that benefits it. The ISP could show its own ads, display its own search results, et cetera.

Since our digital infrastructure doesn't legally require the same over-sight as other essential utilities, the government pays less attention to those issues. The lack of federal oversight and regulation has allowed many ISPs to manipulate online traffic. Adopting the Internet as a public utility will force the federal government's hand to enforce balanced regulations that dismantle the hegemony of selected providers over our collective digital infrastructure landscape.

13

The Role for IT Security Professionals

I began participating in the US-CERT program from nearly its inception. It's been a source of pride for me, working as a private business owner in the cybersecurity field while doing my part as a member of US-CERT to help the government protect our nation's digital infrastructure. Doing so has only reinforced my belief that partnering with the U.S. government to improve cybersecurity also helps to protect my business. As one of those IT experts and private-sector participants monitoring incoming cybersecurity threats all day, every day, I assist in the creation of the patches, solutions, and alerts sent out to the world that are responsible for thwarting plots that threaten both the private and public sectors.

Additionally, I'm a certified member of (ISC)^2, an organization of 150,000 cybersecurity professionals that grants global certification to its members.[1] I, as well as thousands of other IT security professionals, know firsthand just how effective public/private partnerships can be to protect businesses and the public from cyber threats. Maybe it's one of the reasons why as a global business owner with a goal to make money like everyone else, I long ago lost the typical adversarial position with the government.

Operating in the international space as a cybersecurity professional and business owner, I quickly learned that our government is crucial for helping me to conduct business abroad while safeguarding my company from cyber threats. In that capacity, I realized just how much of an ally the U.S. government can be on behalf of American corporations and its citizens. For all of us to come together domestically to combat the DNS threat, those of us in the cybersecurity world with experience working with the government to fight international cyber threats have a crucial role to play in helping to bridge these divides.

One role that IT security professionals can play in securing the DNS is what I'm attempting to do with this book. We have to explain the threat in terms everyone can understand. Public buy-in to any government-backed solution requires plenty of public education. Everyone, from home-based users to CEOs of multinational corporations, must have a basic understanding of the threat we all face in order to combat it.

Once we all have a meeting of the minds about what the threat is, then we can begin to truly come up with viable solutions. Beyond helping to bridge the knowledge gap between corporate and government decision-makers and IT professionals, IT security professionals have to get a seat, at the very least, near the head of the table.

More Online Activity Attracts More DNS Attacks

Remote work and remote schooling aren't the only online activities that have increased exponentially because of COVID-19. Practically all online activity has skyrocketed. Stay-at-home orders across the country in March and April 2020 meant people were ordering everything online from toilet paper and groceries to medicine and COVID-19 personal protective equipment (PPE). As a result, the first two quarters of 2020 saw an uptick of almost $100 billion in online purchases.[2]

Compare that to a typical non-pandemic year and the increase is gob-smacking. According to the Adobe Digital Economy Index, Americans spent the equivalent of 1.6 million years online shopping calculated in hours spent online — a whopping 14 billion hours, and that was in just the first eight months of 2020! The previous year, there were only two non-holiday-season days in which online purchases topped $2 billion. In 2020, by August, there were more than 130 days when online purchases exceeded $2 billion.

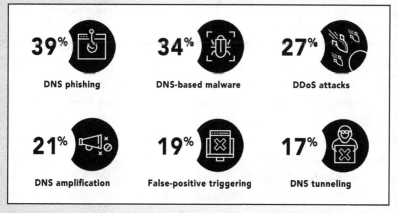

Fig. 13 Top DNS-based attacks suffered.
Source: www.techrepublic.com/article/how-dns-attacks-threaten-organizations.

Just as the move to remote work and education caught the eye of hackers around the world, so did this tsunami of e-commerce activity from nontraditional online consumers. Adding to the incentive for bad actors to attack the DNS was the idea that so much of this new online activity was cloud-based, relying on remote servers hosted by third-party providers.[3]

Cloud providers typically serve customers around the globe. Because of that, cloud-based services generally rely on remote servers to store massive amounts of data. As you now know after reading the first several chapters of this book, servers provide access to root servers and the unencrypted, most insecure part of the DNS. Hackers take advantage of the opportunity to intercept global traffic coming from e-commerce, government, and research institutions by targeting them with increasing DNS attacks.

In 2019, just shy of 80 percent of tech professionals in Europe, Asia, and North America surveyed for the 2020 Global DNS Threat Report said they were hit with DNS attacks. In fact, on average, every participant in the survey suffered more than nine DNS assaults over the year, each one costing nearly $1 million. While phishing emails still remain the gateway for most hacks, the number and type of DNS attacks in recent years have evolved.

Malware implanted in the DNS infrastructure has risen to second behind phishing attacks as the most common DNS-based assaults. SolarWinds and FireEye were victims of malware that exploited vulnerabilities in the authorities governing the DNS. DDoS strikes aren't far behind, and in some attacks, like the one on SolarWinds, there have been combinations of attack methods hitting simultaneously or in a specific order.

Although downtime is reported as the most common result of a DNS attack, that only scratches the surface. Downtime for businesses with time-critical and time-sensitive work can make or break a company. It can cause users to avoid a website for at least a few hours if the system is restored quickly, but there's always the potential to lose customers for good when extended downtime is suffered. And while 16 percent report having sensitive information stolen in a DNS attack, the truth is it's hard to say with some of the more sophisticated DNS attacks just what information was taken.

Apps and IoT devices also provided added layers of vulnerabilities to the overall DNS infrastructure. As Ronan David, vice president of strategy for EfficientIP, puts it, "In this era of key IT initiatives like IoT, Edge, SD-WAN, and 5G, DNS should play a much larger role in the security ecosystem. It offers valuable information that can make security strategies against hackers much more proactive and preventative."[4]

Without Comprehensive DNS Security No Corporate DNS Infrastructure Is Safe

Most IT security professionals work for other people. Whether it's in the corporate boardroom or a federal government agency, IT pros have an up-close view of the vulnerabilities networks face. For corporations that are the most widely targeted in the United States, the risk of DNS attacks is exceedingly high. The lack of preparedness for DNS hacks found in most corporations is only worsened by the fact that there's no comprehensive DNS infrastructure to protect those systems. Recent analysis shows that a full four out of five "companies are at greater risk of compromising their DNS/domain portfolio because they have not adopted basic measures to prevent it."[5]

We know that one of the most insidious methods for attacking the DNS as well as the most dangerous goal is to infiltrate networks by posing as a legitimate registrar or root level authority. Doing so gives hackers the power to act as imposters without detection, altering the fundamental flow of data from legitimate traffic lanes to nefarious ones. As with some ransomware attacks, the goal might not be merely to siphon off millions of dollars from a multi-billion-dollar company but instead to disrupt the global order by blowing up large swaths of the Internet.

In the recent SolarWinds hack, malicious actors created malware that authorities unintentionally implanted in the update systems of one of the United States' most widely used security firms. With Russia backing that attack, who knows how far or how deep the end goal of such a breach was? But what we do know is that "retail-grade" registrars are much more vulnerable to cyberattacks than "enterprise-class" registrars whose accreditation standards and compliance are stricter. Why should any registrar at this point not be required to undergo the types of vulnerability assessments and technical controls that an enterprise-class registrar does?

Meanwhile, hackers are migrating from DDoS attacks and phishing intended to simply siphon off data to almost exclusively going after DNS attack vectors. According to the numbers from Infoblox in 2019, 90 percent of "malware incidents and more than half of all ransomware and data theft attacks" targeted DNS attack vectors.[6] These assaults are no flash in the pan and can have far-reaching consequences.

Take for instance the Dyn attack that occurred in 2016. There, the Internet for the entire Eastern Seaboard of the United States was shut down because of a DDoS strike that exploited Dyn's DNS servers. The threat has only grown more sophisticated and the attacks more complex over the past few years. At the same time, with DoH and DoT moving rapidly forward, the knowable gaps in DNS infrastructure could become even more complicated to protect.

From an IT perspective, that isn't to say there's no role or place for DoH and DoT. It just means that unlike a corporate perception that's mostly motivated by the profits secured from a more lax regulatory environment, or a government outlook that can generally be narrow-minded and far too slow to keep up with threats, DoH and DoT depend on an IT security perspective.[7]

Developing a government solution to the DNS threat has to be comprehensive. Without a comprehensive solution that includes many layers of DNS encryption and security measures, no corporate or government infrastructure is safe. In matters dealing with the technology necessary to combat DNS attacks, it's crucial to rely on the science of the technology behind these assaults and the experts who know something about them.

Confronting the Politics of DNS

Professionals working in the IT industry such as the ones I came up with tend to steer clear of office politics and are completely foreign to national politics. For tech nerds like me, there are no politics to the science — it is what it is. However, in a democracy, in the real world, there are decisions that depend on politicians looking at things through political lenses. IT security pros have to understand the politics behind the politics to make a strong pitch for what's necessary for all people using the Internet globally if we're to keep it stable and functioning for the future.

Politically speaking, there are so-called libertarian views of the Internet, a more laissez-faire approach to regulation. The numbers show that the "all-is-fair" attitude doesn't work for many Americans. It's left tens of millions of them locked out of basic opportunities and has exacerbated a dangerous and growing wealth gap that threatens the underpinnings of democratic society. Frankly, the libertarian approach doesn't cut it. There clearly needs to be some regulation in addition to basic standards and best practices.

Still, it's undeniable that the free and unfettered nature of the Internet has allowed it to blossom into the many positive things it's become. For one, it allows those with access to make a living remotely, affords a quality education online, and enables full-functioning lifestyles without the hassle of a nine-to-five commute. But that's a big *if*, and if you don't have that kind of access, you're cut off from all those things that are essential to daily life in the 21st century.

Google, Twitter, and Facebook corporate executives can't be the arbiters of free speech online. Neither can they be depended on to be the benevolent benefactors of Americans regarding products and services during a time of crisis. At some point, as was the case two months into a multi-year pandemic, these corporate executives are going to return to raising prices for their customers to cover their bottom lines. Therefore, it's incumbent upon the government to step in and make sure Americans are protected, even if that means making certain Internet goods and services are universally available to the public.

Getting Everyone on Board with Government-Controlled Local DNS Servers

Who better to make the case for why local DNS servers controlled by coordinating local, state, and federal agencies is the best way to go than IT experts who have been way ahead of the curve in seeing these threats coming? The technology behind and the ability to layer protection through local DNS servers will require smart architecture built by people who know how to build a secure digital network.

From the very inception of the Internet, the reliance on government and private-sector researchers is the reason why the development of the Internet was and has been such an extraordinary invention. But it isn't just the technology itself; it's what it has become through individual creativity and design. How do we maintain that freedom while also guarding the Internet against those who would dismantle it? It begins with getting everyone on board with the idea of government-controlled local DNS servers. Let's start with getting buy-in from our authorities — the registrars and resolvers, some of whom are already on board with these concepts.

In 2020, one of the main DNS resolvers announced its openness to embracing encryption standards at the authoritative level.[8] Some have suggested that bringing opponents of encryption like ISPs into the fold can be achieved by certifying them as trusted recursive resolvers (TRRs). That would go a long way toward eliminating the threat from DNS imposters attempting to gain credentials at the authorities level. The problem is the lack of faith that corporations agreeing to act as resolvers will also relinquish their access and control to customer data.

That last hurdle is being overcome by corporate partnerships that might further complicate DNS security aims. Take, for example, Comcast's announcement that the cable giant is partnering with Mozilla to encrypt Firefox browsers. By partnering, Comcast has been able to retain its ability to filter content for legal reasons and for parental controls. In doing so, the company has also pledged to respect privacy standards set by Mozilla in order to be granted the ability to act as a TRR for Firefox traffic.[9] The declaration explained that "Adding ISPs in the TRR program paves the way for providing customers with the security of trusted DNS resolution, while also offering the benefits of a resolver provided by their ISP such as parental control services and better optimized, localized results."[10]

Of course, most Americans aren't willing to simply rely on the promise of a company that makes lots of money off the data they promise to stop collecting. How would most users know either way? Data collection happens right now, and users generally have no idea where it's going or what it's being used to do. In order to get public buy-in, empowering government oversight and regulation gives users a voice in the debate and returns control back to the people.

Building Consensus Around Best Practices

As Owen Bennett and Udbhav Tiwari say in a Mozilla blog, "In the early days of the Internet, these kinds of threats to people's privacy and security were known, but not being exploited yet. Today, we know that unencrypted DNS is not only vulnerable to spying but is being exploited, and so we are helping the Internet to make the shift to more secure alternatives."[11]

Worst-case scenario, it takes months if not a couple of years before we actually start implementing any national plan. In the meantime, there are best practices beginning to formulate around securing the DNS on an individual basis. Most individuals use the DNS servers of their ISPs. The majority of businesses now employ third-party cloud services to manage their DNS services. Cloud providers usually provide faster Internet service while proactively protecting against new and evolving DNS attacks.

One practice that needs to be stopped is the redirection of bad queries to ISPs' own ad pages, a practice that some major providers have adopted as a way to increase revenue.[12] Beyond creating more distrust between ISPs and their customers, this also produces an attack vector and another opportunity for customers' queries to be interrupted or intercepted.

Mozilla claims that its move to DoH "helps hide your browsing history from attackers on the network, helps prevent data collection by third parties on the network that ties your computer to websites you visit."[13] Yet, as I've shown, it's by no means standard even with others slowly following suit. But could it be, or rather, should DoH be a new universal standard? From my experience and based on research for this book, here are five best practices I believe we can all support.

1. **Hide Primary Servers:** *It's best to restrict primary nameservers' access to users responsible for maintenance and storing data in those servers, since it helps to ensure DNS data integrity.[14] Any server that hosts the master copy of a zone needs to remain hidden as a primary. The purpose of such servers should be exclusive to supplying data to secondary nameservers across the company. These servers must be made accessible to end users and not be listed as nameservers for any particular zone. Secondary nameservers are responsible for answering queries, which is why primary nameservers accept or respond to any DNS query from an end user. However, if a company has externally available nameservers, the primary nameservers should be configured behind a firewall. If those servers have the right firewall rules in place, the secondary servers can be configured to execute queries and transfers from the primary server.*

2. **Focus on Behavior Analytics from DNS Data:** *The 2020 EfficientIP study mentioned earlier concluded with several recommendations. One that would make a huge difference in protecting individual networks is to, as EfficientIP puts it, "empower Zero Trust." Basically, that means focusing on improving detection by gleaning certain user behaviors from the data coming from DNS security logs. Think of it as a way to customize DNS threat monitoring based on typical client or user behaviors. Anything out of the ordinary should alert whoever's responsible for monitoring the network to investigate.*

3. **Make DNS Security a Part of Network Architecture:** *Speaking of customizing DNS security, a major way to improve it is to infuse it into every aspect of network architecture. Too frequently, DNS is viewed through a narrow prism, concentrating largely on general*

traffic. What about the IoT devices connected to the network of a company or organization? DNS security should include any apps that users in a network are connected to, as well as any devices or third-party Internet services.

4. **Employ Proactive and "Adaptive" DNS Security Measures:** By employing the previous point — infusing the entire architecture with DNS security measures — it's easier to adopt proactive and adaptive measures. When EfficientIP reported the results of the survey conducted by the IDC, nearly every company believed DNS security should be a top priority most used an automated monitoring system. Some things can be automated but not everything, and by designing more "purpose-built" DNS security, automated features of DNS can be made proactive in detecting threats and more adaptive in responding to them.

5. **Establish a "Domain Security Council":** Finally, a big part of the debate once the policy-making stage is reached will be who's in charge: the government, corporations, privacy advocates? How about a smart mix of collaborators? The writers at Security suggest creating something called a "Domain Security Council."[15] Earlier, I noted how many recent DNS attacks targeted easier-to-infiltrate retail-grade registrars. A DSC is meant to deploy "enterprise-class registrars and additional best practices."

The *Security* writers go on to spell out how the "Domain Security Council" would be organized to come up with the best, best practices:

Through such a council, chief information security officers (CISOs) collaborate with corporate C-suite members to identify, implement and continuously monitor/improve upon domain security policies and procedures.

For example, the Chief Compliance Officer would be very keen to understand the risk, and how to rate it. General Counsel would be concerned about IP rights and data privacy due to General Data Protection Regulation (GDPR). A Chief Marketing Officer would want to understand the business impact to a brand in the case of a cyber attack. There can be much at stake requiring a variety of stakeholders to weigh in.[16]

The above points are all up for debate, but we can begin to build consensus around some of the best practices that businesses, individuals, educational institutions, and research and government agencies can implement while local DNS is being worked out and deployed nationwide.

Staying Ahead of DNS Threats

Researchers have already spotted malware built to evade detection by connecting to command-and-control servers using encrypted DNS requests.[17,18] And another major concern is that if hackers compromised a trusted DNS resolver, they would be able to pull off devastating DNS hijackings that wouldn't be detectable to the outside world. A similar issue already exists when hackers compromise the "certificate authorities" that underpin general HTTPS web encryption.[19,20]

Without an equally robust cybersecurity strategy, risks increase dramatically for intrusions, especially since these technologies amass data as well as hold proprietary information that could be targeted by data thieves and corporate spies. On top of that, research and development, customer relationship management, and data analytics typically end up in the purview of marketing professionals as opposed to IT security professionals.

Therefore, IT security professionals play a crucial role in securing the DNS when adopting technologies that are critical for systems to communicate with one another and for network managers to protect them. If IT security professionals aren't involved in the planning or aren't aware of the specific needs of each industry and government agency, how can they be expected to ensure that the entire country's digital infrastructure is protected?

14

Action Plan for DNS Public/Private Partnerships

If an e-commerce site is slow because name resolution is sluggish, sales will be lost. If someone takes over a domain name due to a DNS security flaw, a business can lose everything. If a hack manages to infiltrate a root server for all top level domains (TLDs), well, that's catastrophic to the world. It's such a big deal that it's incredible that it's only just now getting some attention, yet not nearly enough. Few users understand the role of the DNS in their utilization of the Internet, or the potential for widespread abuse of their DNS information.

Going through the effort of explaining what the DNS is and how it works is my way of making sure that, along with decision-makers and cyber experts, users understand the threat we face in addition to the complexity of the solution in a way that can be easily grasped. There's an important reason for this. If users don't comprehend how the DNS works, then we can't make meaningful choices together about how to protect our collective data. The only thing businesses and the public in general care about is that systems work. They want a working website when they click a link. Short of that, they really don't care about the nuts and bolts. I've shown in previous chapters how part of making DNS encryption work is helping all decision-makers as well as users understand what it is and how it works so that we can take the right actions to ensure the stability of the Internet for the future.

Rather than simply detail the problem before us, in this final chapter I'll lay out an action plan that can serve as a roadmap to get the ball rolling on universal Internet access and DNS security through local servers. Clearly, this threat is urgent. The pandemic that revealed the deep systemic disparities in our society also showed the dire consequences that a lack of Internet access can have in a world where everything we do connects to the Internet. In response, there are two important points we have to remember when devising a solution:

1. **We Can Do This:** *The threat I've laid out is daunting, no doubt. We've known about this vulnerability for decades, and it hasn't been fixed in part because of the complexity of the problem. But daunting doesn't mean impossible when we put our heads together. When the pandemic hit, researchers around the world, including America's top minds in epidemiology, raced to create a vaccine to stop the virus. As a result, in less than a year, the world saw multiple vaccines approved for emergency use with 90-plus-percent efficacy and safety ratings. We can put our minds together to do the same for this similarly urgent threat that must be halted as soon as possible.*

2. **Secure Universal Access to the Internet Is Essential and Urgent:** *Early reports on the distribution of COVID-19 vaccines showed that the most affected communities, largely lower-income people and people of color, were getting vaccinated at a fraction of the rate of wealthier people and white people, the same population that fared better than most during the pandemic.[1] Among the many reasons for this particular disparity was that initially, in order to sign up for a vaccine, one had to do so online and then check back often for an appointment. Lack of universal Internet access in America is literally life or death for large portions of society.*

Internet as a Basic Human Right

In reference to the Internet, Franak Viačorka, a Belarusian analyst and nonresident fellow at the Atlantic Council, has said that "The fate of the country has never depended so much on one [piece] of technology."[2] Social media platforms began taking a real reputational hit starting in 2016 when Russia used social media to corrupt democratic elections around the world, including those in the United States. Over the four years of the Trump administration, misinformation and outright lies on social media led to wild conspiracy theories that culminated in an actual coup attempt on the U.S. government by disaffected Republican voters and armed militia gangs. Lack of oversight of and self-regulation by social media platform companies are ongoing problems that perhaps make it harder to remember the ways social media has actually helped promote democracy and human rights.

It was Twitter that aided Egyptians and other North Africans and Middle Easterners to help overthrow authoritarian governments during the 2011 uprisings.[3] For months, from 2019 to 2020 before the pandemic, China made headlines for its treatment of Hong Kong citizens, which led to demonstrations against the Chinese government that became violent.[4] Viral video shared online and through social media brought worldwide attention to those protests as well as to the nine-plus-minute cellphone video of the murder of George Floyd by a Minneapolis cop in 2020.

Sadly, after these uprisings, some government backlashes against the protesters included stripping and disrupting Internet access to citizens. In 2016, the United Nations officially condemned governments denying Internet access to their citizens in response to legitimate peaceful protest. The Human Rights Council resolution goes on to state that "the same rights that people have offline must also be protected online," namely the right to free speech protected for decades under the Universal Declaration of Human Rights.[5]

Unfortunately, not all nations got on board with the condemnation. In fact, China, as well as Russia, refused to agree without the council removing language calling for human-rights protections for Internet access. Therefore, it's not really surprising that more recently Russia has been accused of aiding the Russian-backed ousted president of Belarus, using Internet disruption and denial as a means to shut down opposition and block external news outlets. Accused in 2020 of stealing an election that would have ended his regime, Belarus's president, Alexander Lukashenko, refused to give up power, then shut down the Internet for his citizens. Once again, it was a social media app, Telegram, that allowed protesters in Belarus to bypass the Internet disruptions, resulting in the successful coordination of rallies and protests through the app, despite the government's attempts to block them.[6]

Five years ago, the United Nations officially declared Internet access to be a human right.[7] In reality, in many parts of the developing world, as it is in the United States, there is no universal access, and typically the most vulnerable in our societies are the ones who suffer the most from a lack of it. During the first partial school year under COVID-19, KSBY News in San Luis Obispo, California, highlighted the difficulties that some parents have simply trying to locate reliable Wi-Fi for their children to continue their education remotely.

Especially underscoring this trend is the story of a mother driving her school-age children in her SUV to a nearby Wi-Fi hotspot during a heat wave and running her car engine for air conditioning for an entire school day so her kids could access their basic right to a public education only available remotely with Internet access because of the pandemic.[8]

As Reuters reporter Avi Asher-Schapiro has written, "Some 16 million children, or 30% of all U.S. public school students, lack either an internet connection or a device at home adequate for distance learning, according to the Boston Consulting Group."[9] It's all too clear that far too many American adults and their children are being denied a basic human right through stagnant policy-making and monopolistic business decision-making.

By treating the Internet as a public utility, local, state, and federal DNS servers can be managed and funded like a utility. The argument that government doesn't do Internet well means we need to improve local government capabilities — not throw out the baby with the bathwater. Right now, local governments provide water, but citizens still filter it for contaminants. If we treat hacking like contaminants in water, it can be filtered out.

On the plus side, unlike gas and electric utilities, DNS servers are quite inexpensive to operate. There's no need to meter because a server can be run for an entire city for about $1 per day. In fact, some home routers have DNS servers built in for free. If governments provide some basic level of free Internet connectivity everywhere, that would go a long way to making access universal.

Most airports, libraries, and coffee shops already supply free Wi-Fi, though free Wi-Fi networks tend to be even more vulnerable to the external and fundamental threats facing all Internet connections. Government-provided DNS could offer the same level of accessibility with the added benefit of improved security. Domain registration could be handled at the city level, as is the case with other utilities. Businesses could then be required to register for permits and also enroll their domain names at city hall. That would allow citizens to apply for DNS services through their city's servers.

The way it works now, ISPs assign DNS server addresses. Local governments, however, could force ISPs to use city DNS servers so that when domain query traffic goes out, it moves to city servers that look up locations of websites. In addition to adding more security to Internet queries, a shift like this would improve Internet speeds for everyone, making high-speed access universal, since local DNS servers are faster than faraway, remote ones.

Transitioning from "Natural Monopolies" to Public Goods

When I say that one of the two things we have to remember to focus on is that we can do this, I say it with confidence, because we've accomplished this before — at least something very similar. The United States dealt with the first "natural monopoly" situation in telecommunications in 1913 when telephone pioneer AT&T was allowed by Congress to operate as a monopoly with "favored status" from the government.[10] The difference between then and now is that to receive that favored status AT&T had to agree to regulated service standards and pricing, something current Internet service providers don't do.

Just as the Internet in the United States was allowed to flourish with little to no regulation to give it the time and space to become universal, the phone industry was permitted to operate monopolistically with the blessing of the federal government as a way to create a compatible-technology network for telephone consumers that would be country-wide. The telephone had become an essential good during emergencies. It was no longer a luxury of the wealthy but a means for everyday citizens to get in touch with the police, hospitals, employers, et cetera.

Because of that, the American government limited the ability of AT&T to pocket too much profit for providing universal service. It was allowed to make money but not take advantage of its status in the market — the most glaring difference between then and now. Instead, this investment by the U.S. government to expand AT&T's service to the public was for the public good, so maintaining its equipment and improving its technology were also part of the deal for favored status. However, the Internet has been around since the 1980s, and we're still far from universal status in the United States. I've also discussed previously how our digital infrastructure is in disrepair and outdated.

Not even a decade after the first legislation governing the telecommunication industry, problems with the "natural monopoly" status granted to AT&T became challenging. Senator Willis Graham introduced the Graham Act in 1921, allowing different telephone companies to compete in the same market. The bill, however, passed without that provision and instead institutionalized AT&T's monopoly status, exempting phone companies from antitrust regulations and enabling them to merge into giant noncompetitive corporations.

Being the first gave AT&T the advantage of establishing its equipment and networks across the United States in the same way that some of the earliest mobile providers and ISPs have been able to corner chunks of the market because of their nationwide infrastructure. Like mobile and broadband providers today with the ability to offer coast-to-coast connectivity, only AT&T was able to deliver long-distance service to its customers. That granted it the capacity to continue acting as a monopoly, even as smaller, local phone companies popped up and competed.

It wasn't until 1934, right in the middle of the Great Depression and President Franklin Roosevelt's New Deal, that universal telephone service was officially enacted by Congress. The Communications Act of 1934 granted "rapid, efficient, nation-wide, and world-wide wire and radio communication service with adequate facilities at reasonable charges ... to all the people of the United States." In the face of great economic distress, this was the first law to make universal telephone service a basic public good to be made available coast-to-coast even to people who couldn't afford it.

Fair minds must reasonably concede that Internet service has, in the midst of recent multiple national crises, been revealed to be essential. Continued monopolies controlling Internet access, pricing, and infrastructure have become dangerous to our national security. For the common good and the best interest of national security, the transition from natural monopolies to public goods for the Internet industry has to start immediately.

Policies for Public Financing of Universal Internet Access

All this work — the changes, the investments, and the incentives — are going to cost money. Fortunately, U.S. history again provides a guide on how to do it. As I've shown before, the Internet is fundamentally a natural extension of telephone technology. In the same way that it took both public and private funding for universal phone access to become a reality, we'll need to do the same for universal Internet. A history lesson here will help us devise smarter policies for public financing of universal Internet access.

Remember that monopoly AT&T had over long-distance calling despite the federal government stepping in to regulate the industry? The government also allowed AT&T to charge more for long distance as a means to cover its new costs for expanding coverage nationwide, resulting in nearly 95 percent of Americans having phone access over the next decade. The Communications Act also first established the FCC, which regulates the telecom industry. It's charged with overseeing "all nongovernmental broadcasting, interstate communications, as well as international communication which originate or terminate in the United States."[11]

AT&T was able to continue to grow and make profits while also fulfilling its obligations to the public to supply public pay phones and universal phone lines even in the most remote and rural parts of the United States. It wasn't until the 1980s that the FCC during President Ronald Reagan's administration first instituted the Universal Service Fund (USF) as a way to maintain universal telephone service. Every person who paid for phone service saw a USF charge on his or her phone bill that was there to help fund nationwide phone service.

Why not follow the same model and launch a "Universal Internet Access Fund" or UIAF? By creating the UIAF, Congress could pass a small tax on Internet service to help fund the program. As long as municipalities run their own DNS services to prevent ISP DNS hijacking and use those servers to provide free Wi-Fi access in public spaces, they should be eligible for reimbursements from the federal government.

Despite the success of the Communications Act and the USF for expanding telephone service to the public, the Reagan administration was also notorious for its penchant for deregulation. Telephone service and the Communications Act weren't spared. The FCC's mantra shifted from "social equity" to "economic efficiency."[12] In 1996, the Communications Act was replaced with the Telecommunications Act of 1996, still operating as a means to fund low-income families and remote rural areas with phone service through the USF.

Phone companies were responsible for funding the USF for the public by collecting those fees from long-distance subscribers. Internet companies, however, haven't been made accountable for contributing to the USF. In fact, the majority of homes no longer pay for home phone service. Instead, most people use their mobile phones as their home phones, yet mobile providers don't contribute to the USF. Many people use the Internet as a means to communicate and watch television, yet neither the Telecommunications Act nor the USF has been updated to reflect this new reality.

In other words, there should be plenty of money for a UIAF if we had the laws on the books to keep up with where current technology is instead of relying on outdated laws that don't apply or have gaping holes in the regulatory landscape governing the Internet. Under President Barack Obama's administration, this transition was approved by the FCC in 2011 when the Connect America Fund was created to replace the USF over the span of six years with a price tag of more than $4 billion annually. Since 2009, AT&T, which is also a major cellphone carrier along with Verizon, has been lobbying Congress to force broadband and mobile providers to help fund the USF, specifically as a means to expand service to rural and underserved areas.

Another idea about how to fund universal Internet access is similar to how the Affordable Care Act is funded and how proposed health care for all would work. Every American would receive basic Internet access free.[13] Just as before the transition to digital, if a TV cable was plugged into an outlet, albeit illegally, basic cable could be received without paying for it. People should have basic Internet access, but for faster speeds or to use more data, premium packages would be paid for in the same way they are for cable. Similar to AT&T charging long-distance customers to cover their portion of the USF, users paying for premium packages would be charged a UIAF fee to cover basic service nationwide.

Adding Broadband and Wireless to FCC's Lifeline Program

As further proof that broadband is essential in an emergency, within 10 days of the national shutdown in March 2020 due to the pandemic, the Lifeline program run by the FCC was ordered to keep low-income and rural Lifeline subscribers connected. The Lifeline program has been in place since the Telecommunications Act was enacted and provides very low-priced phone service to qualifying low-income telephone subscribers as well as to some rural subscribers and those living on Tribal Lands.[14]

The order extending waivers on enrollment, certification, usage, and documentation requirements through November 2020 prevented shutoffs of cellphone service and landlines temporarily. With millions facing unemployment because of the closures, the program was also extended for the first time to unemployed people, even if their previous income levels didn't qualify them. Without this emergency service, millions could have been left without a means to call an ambulance if they were sick with COVID-19 or to access online resources for unemployment benefits, online schooling, and relief money.

A full five years before the pandemic, the Obama administration had already expanded the Lifeline program to include mobile service and broadband access. That year, in June 2015, the FCC began work updating and modernizing its Lifeline services. Just short of a year later, the FCC voted to add subsidies for Internet access to the Lifeline program. Here, again, history can be our guide for how to devise funding for Lifeline broadband service.

The simple fact is that if the Internet is a necessity, like power and water, we need clear rules to ensure the greatest possible access at the lowest possible price. ISPs could be charged with delivering Lifeline broadband service based on the appropriate government agencies establishing proof of need to receive reimbursement from the program. Local municipalities could establish local Internet service reimbursements through Lifeline for the entire city through partnerships between local governments and ISPs.

Public/Private Partnerships to Manage Local DNS Servers

All of the players working privately in cyberspace need this change in the digital infrastructure of the United States to protect the Internet. But let's not forget that the majority of people online today access the Internet through their smartphones. Wireless and mobile technology, in conjunction with the IoT and the billions of wireless devices attached to the Internet, are all vulnerable to the same DNS threat.

Early in 2021, Israeli researchers released information about a series of DNS attacks during the summer of 2020 aimed at wireless devices connected to the Internet. Similar to the SolarWinds hit but on a much smaller scale, hackers employed a DNS cache-poisoning assault against a local DNS server called DNSmasq through an open-source software update to the server. The DNSpooq attack attempted to redirect the million or so users of this local server to their "attacker-controlled domain."[15]

While this hack was relatively small, it highlights how enormous the complexity of the problem is when you factor in mobile devices that can also be spoofed, intercepted, or otherwise compromised as a gateway to infiltrate DNS servers. There were more than a dozen downstream and upstream vendors affected by this attack, according to US-CERT, with both it and CISA issuing warnings about this incursion.

Local DNS wouldn't likely use DNSmasq, which is well suited as a DNS server for small networks such as home ones. Bind DNS is the software of choice for most large deployments. All software needs security updates, and DNSmasq is no exception and neither is Bind. As long as patches are applied when security researchers find vulnerabilities, all is well. Yet to stay in front of new and evolving threats circling closer and closer to the Internet's fundamental flaw, confronting any vulnerabilities created by local DNS infrastructure is important as well as considering the role for mobile providers and wireless technology in implementing a secure DNS infrastructure.

Already the future for mobile providers in this new localized DNS infrastructure is currently under way through a new public/private partnership. QUALCOMM, a major wireless company, has joined with a group of other providers to create new, modern-day pay phones. Instead of aiming their program at actual phones, these companies have agreed to pour in close to a quarter of a billion dollars to place wireless hotspots across the country, ones that will cover 150 feet at really high speeds.

In return, half the revenue from ads placed inside these digital kiosks will go to providers, with the other half to local governments. That would mean a profit of $34 million annually for a city — twice as much revenue as derived from antiquated pay phones now. Estimates put the profits over the next dozen years at a billion dollars, more than enough money to help fund local DNS servers and the agencies charged with maintaining and operating them.

Through these public/private partnerships, cable and telecom companies can still compete to provide premium services, as well as vie for government contracts to supply and maintain services. Rather than negatively impacting the industry, public/private partnerships improve it by expanding the reach of the goods and services on the Internet to all people. This is a win for users who can save on their data plans, and it can be a victory for mobile networks that would make more profits while also securing their own networks.

Implementation Plan for Very Local DNS

The main thread that runs through this book is that the DNS is critical to a secure and available Internet. The DNS is often taken for granted and over-looked until it's exploited. Making it secure and reliable should be the first priority for establishing Internet security and privacy at every company and government agency going forward. So how do we do that? We can start by having a government-provided, reliable, and secure DNS server in every local government office. It's inexpensive to operate and provides a large mesh of reliable nameservers to support the country's Internet infrastructure.

After nearly three decades working in cybersecurity and technology, as the owner of a global IT firm, and based on all the research conducted for this book, I've come up with five pillars for implementing a plan for very local DNS:

1. *Free Local Internet Access Through Hotspots:* Local governments should provide free local Internet access like the basic services cable and telecom companies provide today for monthly fees. New York City has already begun a plan to do this over the next eight years.[16] Boston is planning to provide nearly 200 hotspots throughout the city, while Los Angeles hopes to secure a commitment from Internet providers there to offer free basic service to L.A. residents.

2. *Government-Controlled DNS Security:* We can no longer expect private ISPs to take care of the public good, especially when

it comes to DNS security. While some people are leery about trusting local governments to properly protect against DNS threats, these new local DNS servers must be controlled by local governments as part of the broader national digital infrastructure security strategy.

3. **Encrypted Data Going to and from Public Wi-Fi:** As New York City and other major cities start to implement test programs for free public Wi-Fi, security must come first, not only to realize the main goal of fundamentally safeguarding the Internet but also to guarantee public buy-in. Assuring users that these public Wi-Fi networks will be encrypted and anonymized will be crucial in building trust.

4. **Modernized Features at Digital Kiosks:** Cities working on test programs for public Wi-Fi all promise Internet that will be very high speed for free, some 20 times that of average home-based service. Additional features of modern-day pay phones should include rapid charging stations as well as a new version of pay phones for those without devices. All of this can be provided free to the public and easily managed through new local government charters.

5. **Federal Standards Should Guide Local Government Servers:** Part of the funding for implementing very local DNS will come from public/private partnerships, but some of that money will also be supplied by the U.S. government. Since local DNS will be part of the overall national DNS security strategy, new local DNS infrastructure and free Wi-Fi standards should be set and overseen by the federal government.

By simply converting outdated pay phones into working digital kiosks, nationwide Internet access would immediately increase exponentially, providing mobile owners with savings on their data-usage plans. As such, mobile providers and ISPs will amass millions of new customers. These partnerships can be win-win-win solutions to one of our most vexing problems.

What follows are measures to make very local DNS a reality.

New Public DNS Infrastructure

In the same way that our digital security plan has to be diversified with layers of encryption at strategic points to make data more secure in transit, we also have to do the same with our physical DNS infrastructure. There's a correlation between ISPs' DNS servers and electric and gas meters. Every gas and electric meter is decentralized based on region, county, and city, all the way down to the individual apartment or home.

The modern Internet was built from a foundation with layers and layers of individual websites that have expanded it so much that we've actually created a gargantuan system that lends itself to major disruptions and in many ways is as delicate as a game of Jenga. As we formulate strategies to implement public DNS servers, the guiding principle should be that "smaller, local systems which are built to be resilient tend to hold up better under pressure and disruption."[17]

Already individual state governments have experimented with different broadband infrastructure designs. Referred to as the "laboratory of ideas," U.S. states usually take the lead when new technology runs into government operations. However, without federal coordination, they quickly become disparate patchwork systems that create even more attack vectors, resulting in more vulnerabilities. For some states, these changes are merely in response to upgrades to current utility infrastructures such as the federal electricity grid.

Virginia's upgrades give utility providers the ability to add fiber-optic cables. The state then leases those cables to ISPs that can provide their services to businesses and individuals. Tennessee announced a plan to connect every citizen in its state to broadband through a grant program. That came after a statewide initiative to create Tennessee's very own network of fiber-optic cables was proposed more than a decade ago. Less than a decade later, *Consumer Reports* ranked Chattanooga, Tennessee, as the U.S. city with the best broadband in America.[18]

Leveraging Deals with ISPs for Public Broadband

President Eisenhower got the idea for the interstate highway system based on a strategic military need. He saw that our inadequate and crumbling infrastructure made us vulnerable to foreign invasion at a time when the threat of communism and the atomic bomb was everywhere. Similarly, the paltry effort to connect every American as well as the haphazard approach to national digital security have also produced a national security threat. Equally important, America's ability to compete is hindered in a world where our main economic competitors provide faster, better, reliable universal Internet access to all their people.

One way to get the ball rolling is to build new DNS infrastructure by leveraging the power of America's state, local, and federal government contracts to come up with deals. In the same way that Virginia relies on its own government to expand broadband that cuts ISPs out, the state then gives them the chance to come back in by leasing those cables to their customers at a profit.

As I mentioned previously, things like this are happening all over the United States, with local communities leveraging their power to increase free public access to the Internet in schools and local libraries and to set up public hotspots. By opening those contracts to competitive bids, states can make deals that best serve the public.

Funding the Costs for the Construction of Nationwide Public Broadband Access

Funding is a huge part of the move to the Internet as a utility on the front end. However, when all the state and federal grants aimed at doing the same thing are factored in, it's easy to see how a more coordinated national approach to a big chunk of the funding is necessary. Take for instance the ReConnect Grant program aimed at adding broadband to rural areas.[19] This program is managed by the USDA, not the FCC. Many federal grants can be better coordinated so that more states are eligible for the same grant, which would help move expansion, particularly into underserved areas, much faster.

Dealing with Eminent Domain Due to Public Broadband Expansion

Eminent domain is the process by which the federal or state government can seize private property for public use. This happens when wells and gas, oil, and electrical lines are installed. Just as with any other utility, eminent domain is going to be a factor when it comes to connecting the entire country to the Internet. Some states have created a certification program for areas of their states that have worked to "remove or minimize barriers to permitting and access to private property — key factors in building broadband networks."[20] Among them are Indiana, Tennessee, Georgia, and Wisconsin, which have set up what they call "broadband-ready" communities.

Eminent domain fights can be emotional and fraught with bitterness, so it will take a lot of smart planning for areas where rural lands are sacred or utilized for farming. In 2018, the annual federal budget included a provision ordering all states that receive money from it for highways to pick someone to serve as the state's "broadband utility coordinator," charged with managing eminent domain cases arising from broadband expansion.

Coordinating Operations Between State, Local, and Federal Agencies

Public/private partnerships are great, but we also need public/public partnerships to help make very local DNS work. Right now, there are states coordinating their broadband expansion and access efforts with other state and local agencies as well as state-based ISPs and corporations. There needs to be greater coordination between the states and federal agencies charged with overseeing the expansion. That begins and ends with first getting a strong handle on the actual coverage map developed for the public by the government, not by private corporations.

Updating the USF with the UIAF

Perhaps it's time to replace the USF completely with the UIAF, or at the very least, include universal Internet access fees within the USF mandate. Additionally, there needs to be massive updates in how the funding is structured. Right now, telephone operators are mainly responsible for funding the USF, but ISPs and mobile providers are the ones that should be paying the lion's share of it now. How money is collected and how it's distributed based on need and quality of access to fund new universal Internet access are open to debate, but certainly they need to be updated to reflect the telecommunications landscape of today, not the one 40 years ago.

Setting Standards for Universal Internet Access

Internet for Internet's sake isn't the goal here. We need standards that at the minimum are high-tech and of stellar quality. If we create a federal agency charged with marketing and funding high standards and regulations for local DNS service, we could raise tax dollars to make local servers competent by partnering with private digital security firms. It would provide an added layer of safety to local DNS by increasing the capabilities of local government DNS managers and administrators.

There are a number of new standards that have to be set and made universal across the United States. While there's still room for debate about what standards should apply to new universal Internet access, there are several standards that we know we'll need to apply to make universal access a reality. What follows are the top-line standards that I believe have to go into any new DNS expansion plan.

Update the National Broadband Map

First and foremost, to ensure that all Americans no matter where they live have access to high-speed Internet as a public utility, we have to know where Internet connectivity is deficient. Earlier, I wrote about how the FCC relies on private ISPs to determine where to expand service and to establish what's considered "underserved" and "unserved" areas. That has to change. An actual, updated, national broadband map that details where broadband expansion is most lacking and most critical must be created. And a new FCC rule that empowers the federal government to set standards for what qualifies as underserved or unserved has to be the first step.

Set Standards for High Public Internet Speeds

Currently, ISPs consider a community connected if just one household has Internet access. It's self-interested standards like those that can no longer be sustained. Such is the case with Internet speeds. In some parts of the United States, ISPs consider Internet speeds of 25 Mbps fast whereas high-speed standards per ISPs themselves are closer to 100 Mbps or higher. It would cost about $100 billion, according to some estimates, to "create a publicly owned broadband network" that offers 100 Mbps for basic universal Internet access.[21] Funding should be tied to whether or not an ISP is actually delivering high-speed Internet.

Protect Internet Access for Vulnerable Citizens in Emergencies

Due to the pandemic, Americans received an up-close and personal glimpse into how necessary Internet access is in an emergency. Access to phone service is largely tied up in broadband and wireless technology for many Americans. When businesses shut down in March 2020, millions of people were laid off, losing their income and thus their ability to continue to pay for phone and Internet at a time when both were critical for staying connected to the outside world.

In light of that emergency, a number of measures were taken to protect Internet access for vulnerable citizens. One way was to place a moratorium on service shutoffs. That happens many times in weather crises for gas and electric service. Now we have to make the same allowances for Internet access. As part of a new UIAF or updated USF, a provision could be included that raises funds through an "emergency broadband connectivity fund."[22]

In turn, federal and state governments can provide subsidies to help ISPs protect network infrastructures in an emergency. During the pandemic, it was left to private corporations to voluntarily provide uninterrupted service to their customers amid the initial lockdown. The FCC secured the "voluntary" pledges of 700-plus private corporations in the telecommunications sector that they wouldn't shut anyone off during the pandemic. In reality, some were cut off, anyway. Verizon signed the pledge, but there were reports that some of its customers laid off during the pandemic were shut off. Subsequently, the company made a public statement that put the onus on its customers, stating, "Customers need to proactively reach out to us to seek relief."[23]

That bit of news sparked a backlash in Congress with bills introduced to punish ISPs and telecom companies through fines if they cut anyone's service anywhere from six months to a year after the national emergency was declared on March 11, 2020. Changes to the FCC under its chairman, Ajit Pai, relinquished the ability of the agency to force ISPs and telecoms to keep service going for affected customers. None of the bills were passed, and ISPs and telecoms went back to charging customers less than two months after the emergency was declared, though the need remained. Obviously, these rules can no longer be "voluntary," and there has to be legislation to codify how ISPs and telecoms are legally obligated to respond in emergencies as well as how the federal and state governments will compensate them for their services.

Expand Internet Access for Students in K-12

Finally, America's schoolchildren took a big and lasting hit during 2020. As was highlighted at the beginning of this chapter, the right to free public education was hindered because of the pandemic. Without Internet access, many K-12 students were unable to access the resources necessary to receive a quality public education. Moreover, beyond connectivity, a large portion of low-income homes in America don't even have computers or tablets for remote learning. These protections have to be built into the foundation of a new universal right to Internet access in the United States.

A Tale of Two New Worlds

The year 2020 is one that will live in infamy. After a year of devastating grief and death, economic collapse, and general unrest, Americans were hopeful that 2021 would be an improvement. Then, not even a week into the new year, there was an insurrection attack on the U.S. Capitol — not from a foreign invader, which is what happened in 1814 when the British Army set fire to the Capitol and White House but from Americans themselves, who turned the world upside down for more than five hours as the country and the world watched in horror.

Next, barely making it to February 2021, three massive snowstorms covered the majority of the United States. From coast-to-coast, states north to south were blanketed in snow and ice and plagued with freezing temperatures. Storms of that nature, though rare, have been occurring with much more frequency, prompting the federal government to weatherize the national energy grid more than a decade ago. Texas experienced a record freeze that predated the 2021 snowstorm exactly a decade ago. Back then, both state and federal agencies recommended that Texas weatherize its energy sector to prepare for increasingly severe weather events due to climate change. The state government did nothing and instead opted to remove its citizens from the national electricity grid — that is, all except El Paso.[24]

Being part of a regional grid that's backed by the national grid, El Paso was prepared for worse weather than what the state saw in 2011. The vast majority — 90 percent of Texans — rely on a state conglomerate of private oil and gas companies that manage the state's utilities. Because of that, those companies were able to choose not to weatherize. The reason for leaving the national grid was to avoid paying tax increases to fund the weatherization project.

As a result, millions of Texans were without heat and electricity in subfreezing temperatures for a week in some places, leading to deaths, hospitalizations, and trauma. Burst frozen pipes caused spikes in gas prices and shortages not just because of the un-weatherized piping but because of unsafe icy roads and snowy bridges. This happened on top of the continuing pandemic in the same month when deaths in the United States reached the half-million mark.

The year 2021 didn't start off with the kind of bang Americans were hoping for, but it did offer a choice. We've seen the stark results of the consequences from decisions we make in our government. Like those epidemiologists who warned us decades ago about the inevitability of future pandemics, like the climate scientists who alerted us three decades ago about global warming, cybersecurity experts have known for decades about this threat and are now warning the world that the vultures are circling.

The results could be global catastrophe. The choice we have to make is clear: which new world will we choose?

Essential Terms We Need to Know (DNS Cheat Sheet)

Comprehending the nuts and bolts of the Domain Name System (DNS) starts with understanding the unique terms used to describe the different operations involved in connecting IP addresses to Internet queries. To make it as simple to understand as possible, I've broken this list into two sections. The first has terms that define the basic rudimentary process of how the DNS works. Using the word puzzle we first saw in Chapter 3 and repeated here, no matter how well or unwell versed any readers are, the roles of these different aspects of the DNS will be easy to digest and conceptualize.

Fig. 14 Fruit Word Scramble.
Source: Courtesy of www.activityvillage.co.uk/fruit-word-scramble. Copyright © 2020 Activity Village. All rights reserved.

Understanding the Root Function of the DNS

Let's start with the elephant in the room — the Domain Name System.

Caching: Once the Domain Name System has resolved a search query, that information is then stored in a cache file for future use. In the puzzle example on this page, all of the matches made from the unscrambled list of fruits to the scrambled list will be stored so that future queries involving any of the words on the list can be accessed locally without the need to go through nameservers and resolvers.

Domain Name System (DNS): This is the mechanism that allows networked computers to connect IP addresses to words that users can read and understand. In our analogy, the DNS isn't just the individual word puzzle; it's the entire book. It's the publisher that prints the book and comes up with the unscrambled and scrambled words.

Domain Registration: Registry operators (ROs) are responsible for maintaining the database of registered domains on the Internet under a specific top level domain (TLD). There's an RO that holds the master database for all websites registered under the *.com* TLD and one that oversees and provides registration of the *.edu* TLD, and so on and so forth. Any registered domain can be looked up through the website of the Internet Corporation for Assigned Names and Numbers (ICANN).[1] ROs support each specific TLD nameserver as well as create and maintain zone files for each TLD. In our analogy, think of the domain registration as the publisher (Activity Village) that makes and publishes the puzzle. Its offices sustain the lists for all the puzzles it's published with all the words in its puzzle database.

Internet Protocol (IP) Address: The IP is the numerical address of each website. The *IP* in IP address stands for Internet protocol. Each active website on the Internet has a unique IP address. In the word puzzle example on the previous page, each scrambled word is an IP address.

Nameservers: I've already written about nameservers at length, but what I've related bears repeating, since they're one of the two essential components of the DNS. Nameservers are computers located all over the planet where all the information needed to connect an IP address with a query is housed. It's the list of unscrambled words in the puzzle, able to see the letters *g-o-a-n-e-r* and translate them into numbers that lead the nameserver to the appropriate unscrambled match.

If a nameserver can't find the information on its server, it will then redirect the request for *goaner* to another server that might contain the match. It might go through a series of servers, and some websites designate where to redirect if the search query isn't found. It's like looking for the unscrambled word for a piece of fruit that isn't on the list. The nameserver will see if the fruit being searched for is listed in some other puzzle.

Regional Internet Registries (RIRs): The RIR is where each IP address is registered. The website owner maintains the authority over that particular domain once it's registered. In our analogy, the RIR is the cheat sheet in the back of the puzzle book that shows each word on the scrambled list connected to the correct word on the unscrambled list. The website will be registered under the TLD registrar as a *.com* or *.net* website, for example. Already there's been an attack on the DNS registrar held by PCH.

Resolvers: Working in tandem with nameservers, resolvers help to orchestrate the search for missing words. Resolvers have a head start in each search based on the "root node" and the last letters of the URL or the TLD name (i.e., *.com, .net, .org,* et cetera). Resolvers may look in local caches, root servers, or nameservers to resolve the query. Once they've made the connection and the data is cached, it's now part of the resolvers' "memory," so to speak, and they won't need to search root servers for the same query the next time.

Some websites make the connection faster by configuring a resolving nameserver that's solely responsible for searching for nearby servers that might have information that hasn't previously been requested and isn't in the user's PC or browser cache. ISPs provide these servers when an Internet service is purchased.

Zone Files: Using the word puzzle analogy again, a new web domain when it's registered sends a text file to be added to the nameservers. This text file shows all the scrambled words with the line drawn to the unscrambled word. It's basically a map showing how each search query connects to the IP address in that domain. When a specific search query is done and the nameserver is accessed, it refers to the zone files to return the information requested quickly.

Understanding the Hierarchy of the DNS

To understand the challenges of securing the DNS, we have to understand the depth of the Internet's DNS hierarchy. For this analogy, it's best to think of the architecture of the DNS as an upside-down tree. The following terms define the different layers, branches, and leaves on the tree all the way to the root.

Fig. 15 The DNS begins with the root (and root servers). Top level domains (TLDs) such as *.net* and *.com* make up the center of the DNS. Domain names can have many subdomains.
Source: www.infoblox.com/dns-security-resource-center/dns-security-overview.

Hosts: A hostname or host is the main name of the website being accessed. It's the *google* in *www.google.com*. Website owners with control over that domain can break out the hostname into different categories as they please, as long as each one is unique. It's the reason why we don't necessarily have to type the *www.* in the URL anymore. Just typing *google.com* still gets to *www.google.com*. That's because both constructs have been created by the domain owner. The hostname can also be altered to direct users to different parts of a website, as in, say, the domain owner of *www.purdue.edu*, which can create a separate hostname under the same domain to direct a user to its history department: *www.history.purdue.edu*.

Local DNS: Besides being the fundamental argument of this book, in general terms, the local DNS is an IT engineering term referring to the closest DNS server, i.e., the local is the location of the DNS server, not a specific city or state.

Namespace: The namespace is the whole tree. In the DNS hierarchy, it's the internal organization of the individual names in a particular domain. The top level domain (TLD) is the branch; the labels are the twigs on each branch; the names are the leaves (also called end nodes) on each twig.

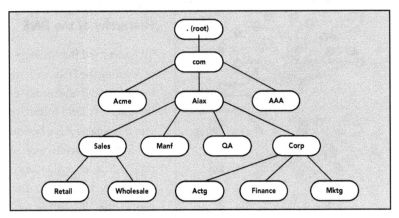

Fig. 16 The DNS hierarchy consists of the root, top level domains (.*com*, for example), domain names (such as *acme.com*), and subdomains (such as *retail.sales. ajax.com*), starting from the bottom left in this illustration and tracing upward.

Source: https://docs.oracle.com/cd/E19455-01/806-1387/6jam692f0/index.html

Resource Records (RRs): In the namespace, each set of records, including IP addresses and email routes (each branch and all of the corresponding leaves on that branch), is grouped as one resource record (RR). Essentially, RRs contain the complete DNS information for each unique resource. Each resource record is defined by six specific types of data, along with a standard classification field:

- Class.
- Name.
- RD Length.
- RData.
- Time to Live (TTL).
- Type.

The RData, RD Length, and TTL classification should be further explained. Each resource record includes a unique RData field that can generally be thought of as the resulting target of the resolved name query. The RD Length is the number of octets in the RData field. Behind the scene, the website builder or administrator uses the TTL to define how long in seconds a particular server should cache (store) a certain resource record. A zero TTL implies that a server shouldn't cache the RR. A short TTL implies that the IP address will likely change soon (think when a system is being migrated or changed in some way). A long TTL tells the server to hang on to that RR, since the IP address isn't expected to change any time soon.

One example of an RR might be:

- <NAME> Wholesale.sales.ajax.com.
- <TYPE> CNAME.
- <CLASS> IN (Internet).
- <TTL> 86400 (seconds in a day).
- <RD Length> 15.
- <RDATA> testing.ajax.com.

Computers receiving this data would know that *wholesale.sales.ajax.com* is an alias for *testing.ajax.com*. A new lookup for "where can I find testing.ajax.com" would happen, as a result. In the search above, attempting to access the wholesale page of the *ajax.com* website, *wholesale.sales.ajax.com* would have its own RR. The details of the RR are useful for DNS systems administrators — and frankly, quite boring for everyone else.

Root Nodes: The earliest version of the Internet used network nodes to map individual network hostnames and databases, that is, until user control created way too many network nodes to work properly. When IP/TCP and the DNS took over, nodes found a new place in the hierarchy. On the DNS tree, the root node is the place where the branch connects to the trunk of the tree. Off that branch grow the twigs that lead to the leaves — the end node or specific webpage in the domain. Root nodes are parent nodes. There can be no siblings or parents, only children that branch off into twigs along the branch.

Root Servers: If we think of the DNS as a tree, at the very top are 13 root servers that serve the entire globe. All are managed and maintained by ICANN, but because of the enormous traffic hitting these root servers, there are identical servers that mirror them. The root servers know all. They have access to all 370 billion domains and the corresponding IP address for each. However, they don't do the work that nameservers and resolvers perform. If a query struggles to find a specific request through nameservers or cache and zone files, it goes to the root servers to get pointed in the right direction, where standard nameservers and resolvers can better locate the request.

Second Level Nodes: When a drawer in a filing cabinet is opened, file folders are found. For computers, these are the second level nodes. Inside the file folders is more specific information contained in the file drawer in this particular filing cabinet.

Subdomain: Also known as a second level domain (SLD), subdomains are under the control of their TLDs. Think of the TLD as the branch and the SLD as the twigs on the branch. There can be many different twigs shooting out that one branch. The *.edu* TLD is a perfect example in which the website is broken into subsections.

Tech Radar uses the example of a school that has a subdomain for its history department. In an SDL construct, the subdomain — in this case the word *history* — will precede the domain name (Purdue, for example) and will end in the *.edu* TLD. Business websites do the same thing with different parts of their business services.

Top Level Domains (TLDs): Everyone who uses the Internet is familiar with TLDs, even if they don't know them as top level domains. Every URL ends with *.something*. The *.something* is the TLD, and it gives the user (and the nameserver) a clue what the user is looking for in a query. For instance *.edu* is an overarching TLD that has a bunch of subdomains. Since it's used by institutions of learning, most college and university websites end in *.edu*, giving the nameserver an idea where to start a search for an address ending in *edu*.

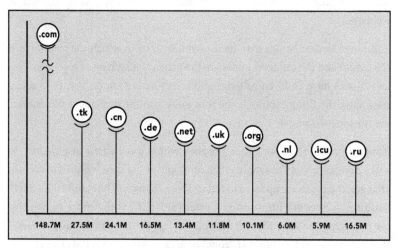

Fig. 17 The top 10 largest top level domains by the number of reported domain name registrations in the second quarter of 2021.

Source: www.verisign.com/en_US/domain-names/dnib/index.xhtml.

In 1984, when the DNS first came online, there were only seven TLDs. Today, there are dozens, including two-letter country domains such as *.cn* for Canada and *.uk* for the United Kingdom. Although ICANN oversees and manages all TLDs, certain entities are granted control by ICANN to manage their own TLDs (governments, for instance), but they still must register their domains with a registry operator (RO).

Top Level Domain Servers: TLD servers are also known as domain level servers and are similar to root servers in that they're at the top of the tree of TLDs, just under the root server. When a TLD searches for a specific *.com* address, it doesn't look through any other TLDs for that information. It just pulls from information contained on the TLD server — all *.com* TLD domains, including the SLDs for those domains.

In Fig. 16, if we try to get to the webpage on the *ajax.com* website for its wholesale department, the root nameserver contacts the *.com* TLD nameserver looking for *ajax.com*. When the branch (TLD) *ajax* is found, it branches off onto the *sales* and *retail* twigs, but only the *sales* twig leads to the *wholesale* leaf (end node) that a user is trying to view.

The namespace also eliminates the need for users to consider lower- and upper-case letters in a search query. Whether searching for *ARPANet*, *ARPANET*, or *arpanet*, all three versions of the spelling are included in the "depth tree" for the website, enabling the resolver to return the correct webpage.

Top Level Nodes: Nodes have their own hierarchy in which the root node is the parent and the top level nodes are the primary offspring or top twigs. Top level nodes have children or twigs and leaves branching off them. To mix a metaphor, the filing cabinet is the root node and the individual file drawers are the top level nodes.

Zones: In addition to zone files, the zone within a domain is also defined to make accessing that data more efficient. If any of the data within the domain changes, the zones are updated to reflect those changes. The Stanford Research Institute — Network Information Center (SRI-NIC) is the entity responsible for managing the zone files for all TLDs except country ones and distributes that data to servers within that "zone" or area of data within the DNS system. Basically, it points the user to the ballpark where the data sought may reside.

Notes

Introduction

1. Rani Molla, "Working from Home Can Make People More Productive, Just Not During a Pandemic," Vox Recode, March 20, 2020, www.vox.com/2020/3/20/21187469/work-from-home-coronavirus-productivity-mental-health-nicholas-bloom.

2. The term *DNSpionage* was coined by Cisco, the U.S. multinational technology conglomerate based in San Jose, California. Cisco used it in November 2018 to describe a massive attack on DNS servers in Lebanon and the United Arab Emirates (UAE).

Chapter 1: Pandemic Proves "Internet Is Essential"

1. Tara Law, "Americans Are Being Encouraged to Work from Home During the Coronavirus Outbreak: For Millions, That's Impossible," *Time*, March 9, 2020, https://time.com/5797382/coronavirus-remote-work-home.

2. Russ Wiles, "Working from Home: Businesses Embrace Telecommuting Amid Coronavirus Outbreak," *Arizona Republic*, March 13, 2020, www.azcentral.com/story/money/business/economy/2020/03/13/working-home-businesses-embrace-telecommuting-coronavirus-outbreak/5033958002.

3. Meghan McCarty Carino, "Remote Work Is Having a Moment Amid COVID-19 Fears," *Marketplace*, March 2, 2020, www.marketplace.org/2020/03/02/remote-work-is-having-a-moment-amid-covid-19-fears.

4. U.S. Bureau of Labor Statistics: www.bls.gov/news.release/flex2.t01.htm.

5. Shelby Livingston, "Highmark Health Sends 8,000 Employees to Work from Home Amid COVID-19 Pandemic," March 16, 2020, www.modernhealthcare.com/insurance/highmark-health-sends-8000-employees-work-home-amid-covid-19-pandemic.

6. Paige Pfleger, "The Coronavirus Outbreak and the Challenges of Online-Only Classes," March 13, 2020, www.npr.org/2020/03/13/814974088/the-coronavirus-outbreak-and-the-challenges-of-online-only-classes.

7. Emily Bary, "'This Is Online Education's Moment' as Colleges Close During Coronavirus Pandemic," *MarketWatch*, March 18, 2020, www.marketwatch.com/story/this-is-online-educations-moment-as-colleges-close-during-coronavirus-pandemic-2020-03-17.

8. "Coronavirus Will Change the World Permanently: Here's How," *Politico*, March 19, 2020, www.politico.com/news/magazine/2020/03/19/coronavirus-effect-economy-life-society-analysis-covid-135579.

9. David E. Sanger and Nicole Perlroth, "Russian Criminal Group Finds New Target: Americans Working at Home," *New York Times*, June 25, 2020, www.nytimes.com/2020/06/25/us/politics/russia-ransomware-coronavirus-work-home.html.

10. Sanger and Perlroth, "Russian Criminal Group Finds New Target."

11. "Russian Hackers Targeting Americans Working from Home During Pandemic," *NBC Nightly News*, June 26, 2020, www.nbcnews.com/nightly-news/video/russian-hackers-targeting-americans-working-from-home-during-pandemic-86080069991.

12. Madison Hoff, "Working from Home Could Be Much Harder Depending on Where You Live: Here Are the 17 US Cities with the Worst Internet Access," *Insider*, April 9, 2020, www.businessinsider.com/us-cities-with-lowest-share-of-computer-and-broadband-internet-2020-3.

13. Zoya Weir, "Best States for Internet Access," *U.S. News*, June 17, 2021, www.usnews.com/news/best-states/slideshows/10-best-states-for-internet-access.

14. Michael Melia, Jeff Amy, and Larry Fenn, "AP: 3 Million US Students Don't Have Home Internet," Associated Press, June 10, 2019, https://apnews.com/article/7f263b8f7d3a43d6be014f860d5e4132.

Chapter 2: The Orgs That Created (and Control) the Internet

1. Tibi Puiu, "Who Really Invented the Internet?" *ZME Science*, February 11, 2020, www.zmescience.com/science/who-invented-the-internet-05264.

2. Puiu, "Who Really Invented the Internet?"

3. Walter Frick, "Who Controls the Internet?" *Harvard Business Review*, June 2016, https://hbr.org/2016/06/who-controls-the-internet.

4. See www.internetsociety.org.

5. The World Summit on the Information Society (WSIS) mandated the secretary-general of the United Nations to convene the global Internet Governance Forum (IGF) for multi-stakeholder policy dialogue. The convening of the IGF was announced by the secretary-general of the United Nations on July 18, 2006: www.intgovforum.org/multilingual.

6. Robert Sanders, "The U.S. Government No Longer Controls the Internet," *Insider*, October 4, 2016, www.businessinsider.com/the-us-government-no-longer-controls-the-internet-2016-10.

7. Susmita Baral, "Who Controls the Internet? US Government Hands over Control to ICANN," *International Business Times*, October 3, 2016, www.ibtimes.com/who-controls-internet-us-government-hands-over-control-icann-2425491.

8. Robert Sanders, "The U.S. Government No Longer Controls the Internet," *Insider*, October 4, 2016, www.businessinsider.com/the-us-government-no-longer-controls-the-internet-2016-10.

9. Packet Clearing House (PCH) provides operational support and security to critical Internet infrastructure, including exchange points and the core of the DNS. See www.pch.net.

Chapter 3: The ARPANET's Achilles' Heel

1. Paul V. Mockapetris and Kevin J. Dunlap, "Development of the Domain Name System," *Computer Communication Review* 18, no. 4 (August 1988): 123–33, http://nms.lcs.mit.edu/6829-papers/dns.pdf.

2. Mockapetris and Dunlap, "Development of the Domain Name System."

3. Verisign, "The Verisign Domain Name Industry Brief," Q1, 2021, www.verisign.com/en_US/domain-names/dnib/index.xhtml.

4. Samantha Lloyd, "Behind the Internet: The History of Domain Names," *TechRadar*, August 13, 2019, www.techradar.com/news/behind-the-internet-the-history-of-domain-names.

5. Danny Palmer, "MyDoom: The 15-Year-Old Malware That's Still Being Used in Phishing Attacks in 2019," *ZDNet*, July 26, 2019, www.zdnet.com/article/mydoom-the-15-year-old-malware-thats-still-being-used-in-phishing-attacks-in-2019.

6. Radware, "Mydoom," *DDoSPedia* (2021), https://security.radware.com/ddos-knowledge-center/ddospedia/mydoom.

7. Boyan Lazarevski, "Anatomy of a DNS Cache Poisoning Attack," Open Web Application Security Project (2019), https://owasp.org/www-chapter-ghana/assets/slides/DNS_Cache_Poisoning(OWASP_GHANA).pdf.

Chapter 4: Crash Course in Current DNS Security

1. Hayley Peterson, "Target Hit by a Major Black Friday Data Breach Involving Customers' Credit Card Information," *Insider*, December 18, 2013, www.businessinsider.com/target-investigating-black-friday-data-breach-2013-12.

2. Brian Melley and Michael Balsamo, "North Korean Charged in Crippling Sony Hack, WannaCry Virus," *AP News*, September 18, 2018, https://apnews.com/article/north-america-hacking-ap-top-news-north-korea-movies-bd7a78e3a1b745b686afd9924a1b9778.

3. See www.blackhat.com/html/webinars/kaminsky-DNS.html for the Black Hat conference presentation. Also available on YouTube.

4. Dan Goodin, "A DNS Hijacking Wave Is Targeting Companies at an Almost Unprecedented Scale," *Ars Technica*, January 10, 2019, https://arstechnica.com/information-technology/2019/01/a-dns-hijacking-wave-is-targeting-companies-at-an-almost-unprecedented-scale.

5. Sara Jelen, "The Top 5 Best DNS Servers for Improving Online Privacy & Security," *SecurityTrails*, April 15, 2020, https://securitytrails.com/blog/dns-servers-privacy-security.

6. Geoff Huston, "Scaling the Root of the DNS," *The ISP Column*, September 2020, www.potaroo.net/ispcol/2020-09/root.html.

7. Dan Goodin, "Inside the DNSpionage Hacks That Hijack Domains at an Unprecedented Scale," *Ars Technica*, February 18, 2019, https://arstechnica.com/information-technology/2019/02/inside-the-dnspionage-hacks-that-hijack-domains-at-an-unprecedented-scale.

8. Avi Kak, "Lecture 17: DNS and the DNS Cache Poisoning Attack," Purdue University, June 25, 2021, https://engineering.purdue.edu/kak/compsec/NewLectures/Lecture17.pdf.

9. Mockapetris and Dunlap, "Development of the Domain Name System," 123–33.

10. Mockapetris and Dunlap, "Development of the Domain Name System," 123–33.

11. Mark K. Lottor, "Internet Growth (1981–1991)," January 1992, https://tools.ietf.org/html/rfc1296.

12. Nick Sullivan, "DNSSEC: An Introduction," *Cloudflare Blog*, October 7, 2014, https://blog.cloudflare.com/dnssec-an-introduction.

13. Brian Krebs, "DDoS on Dyn Impacts Twitter, Spotify, Redditt," *KrebsOnSecurity*, October 21, 2016, https://krebsonsecurity.com/2016/10/ddos-on-dyn-impacts-twitter-spotify-reddit.

14. Brian Krebs, "A Deep Dive on the Recent Widespread DNS Hijacking Attacks," *KrebsOnSecurity*, February 18, 2019, https://krebsonsecurity.com/2019/02/a-deep-dive-on-the-recent-widespread-dns-hijacking-attacks.

Chapter 5: The DNS Threat Assessment

1. Mark E. Jeftovic, "Turns Out Half the Internet Has a Single-Point-of-Failure Called 'Cloudflare,'" EasyDNS, July 20, 2020, https://easydns.com/blog/2020/07/20/turns-out-half-the-internet-has-a-single-point-of-failure-called-cloudflare.

2. Owen Bennett and Udbhav Tiwari, "Mozilla DNS over HTTPS (DoH) and Trusted Recursive Resolver (TRR) Comment Period: Help Us Enhance Security and Privacy Online," *Mozilla Blog*, November 18, 2020, https://blog.mozilla.org/netpolicy/2020/11/18/doh-comment-period-2020.

3. Mark E. Jeftovic, "DOS Attacks and DNS: How to Stay Up If Your DNS Provider Goes DOWN," EasyDNS, August 19, 2010, https://easydns.com/blog/2010/08/19/dos-attacks-and-dns-how-to-stay-up-if-your-dns-provider-goes-down.

4. Ponemon Institute, "Assessing the DNS Security Risk," October 2018, www.infoblox.com/wp-content/uploads/infoblox-whitepaper-assessing-the-dns-security-risk.pdf.

5. Ponemon Institute, "Assessing the DNS Security Risk."

6. Ponemon Institute, "Assessing the DNS Security Risk."

7. Ponemon Institute, "Assessing the DNS Security Risk."

8. US-CERT is a division of the United States Cybersecurity and Infrastructure Security Agency (CISA): https://us-cert.cisa.gov.

9. Ponemon Institute, "Assessing the DNS Security Risk."

10. Ponemon Institute, "Assessing the DNS Security Risk."

11. Ponemon Institute, "Assessing the DNS Security Risk."

12. Infoblox, "What Is a Data Exfiltration?" (2020), www.infoblox.com/glossary/data-exfiltration.

13. Ponemon Institute, "Assessing the DNS Security Risk."

14. Ponemon Institute, "Assessing the DNS Security Risk."

15. Ponemon Institute, "Assessing the DNS Security Risk."

16. Ponemon Institute, "Assessing the DNS Security Risk."

Chapter 6: DNS Security Vulnerabilities and Impact on Internet Infrastructure

1. Darrell Etherington and Kate Conger, "Large DDoS Attacks Cause Outages at Twitter, Spotify, and Other Sites," *TechCrunch*, October 21, 2016, https://techcrunch.com/2016/10/21/many-sites-including-twitter-and-spotify-suffering-outage.

2. Krebs, "DDoS on Dyn Impacts Twitter, Spotify, Redditt."

3. Nicky Woolf, "DDoS Attack That Disrupted Internet Was Largest of Its Kind in History," *The Guardian*, October 26, 2016, www.theguardian.com/technology/2016/oct/26/ddos-attack-dyn-mirai-botnet.

4. Emergency Management & Safety Solutions, "Dyn's Statement About Friday's Historic DDoS Attack," October 23, 2016, https://ems-solutionsinc.com/dyns-statement-about-fridays-historic-ddos-attack.

5. Alex Hinchcliffe, "DNS Tunneling: How DNS Can Be (Ab)Used by Malicious Actors," Palo Alto Networks, March 15, 2019, https://unit42.paloaltonetworks.com/dns-tunneling-how-dns-can-be-abused-by-malicious-actors.

6. Casey Crane, "Re-Hash: The Largest DDoS Attacks in History," *Hashed Out*, June 25, 2020, www.thesslstore.com/blog/largest-ddos-attack-in-history.

7. Krebs, "A Deep Dive on the Recent Widespread DNS Hijacking Attacks."

8. Muks Hirani, Sarah Jones, and Ben Read, "Global DNS Hijacking Campaign: DNS Record Manipulation at Scale," FireEye, January 10, 2109, www.fireeye.com/blog/threat-research/2019/01/global-dns-hijacking-campaign-dns-record-manipulation-at-scale.html.

9. Infoblox, "Solving Unintended Challenges with DoT and DoH" (2021), www.infoblox.com/wp-content/uploads/infoblox-solution-note-dot-and-doh-present-new-challenges.pdf.

10. Benjamin Caudill, "Introducing CFire: Evading Cloudflare Security Protections," Rhino Security Labs, n.d., https://rhinosecuritylabs.com/cloud-security/cloudflare-bypassing-cloud-security.

11. Dominik Tarnowski, "What Are Web Sockets?" February 15, 2017, https://medium.com/@td0m/what-are-web-sockets-what-about-rest-apis-b9c15fd72aac.

12. Open Web Application Security Project (OWASP) Foundation, "Server Side Request Forgery"(2020), https://owasp.org/www-community/attacks/Server_Side_Request_Forgery.

13. Netmeister.org., "DNS Security: Threat Modeling DNSSEC, DoT and DoH," October 10, 2019, www.netmeister.org/blog/doh-dot-dnssec.html.

14. Caudill, "Introducing CFire: Evading Cloudflare Security Protections."

15. Caudill, "Introducing CFire: Evading Cloudflare Security Protections."

Chapter 7: Controversy Around Encrypted DNS

1. Bert Hubert, "Goodbye DNS, Goodbye PowerDNS!" *PowerDNS Technical Blog*, November 27, 2020, https://blog.powerdns.com/2020/11/27/goodbye-dns-goodbye-powerdns.

2. Infoblox, "Solving Unitended Challenges with DoT and DoH."

3. The Internet Engineering Task Force (IETF) is a large, open international community of network designers, operators, vendors, and researchers concerned with the evolution of Internet architecture and its smooth operation. See www.ietf.org/about/who.

4. There are 297 RFCs relevant to the DNS, of which 108 are selected by filter. Total pages selected: 2,082 (https://powerdns.org/dns-camel).

5. John D. McKinnon and Robert McMillan, "Google Draws House Antitrust Scrutiny of Internet Protocol," *Wall Street Journal*, September 20, 2019, www.wsj.com/articles/google-draws-house-antitrust-scrutiny-of-internet-protocol-11569765637.

6. *Slashdot*, "Google's DNS-Over-HTTPS Plans Scrutinized by US Congress," September 29, 2019, https://tech.slashdot.org/story/19/09/29/2033247/googles-dns-over-https-plans-scrutinized-by-us-congress.

7. Timothy B. Lee, "Why Big ISPs Aren't Happy About Google's Plans for Encrypted DNS," *Ars Technica*, Sepember 30, 2019, https://arstechnica.com/tech-policy/2019/09/isps-worry-a-new-chrome-feature-will-stop-them-from-spying-on-you.

Chapter 8: Controversy Around Encrypted DNS — DNSSEC

1. Cathy Almond and Brian Conry, "CVE-2008-1447: DNS Cache Poisoning Issue ('Kaminsky Bug')," Internet Systems Consortium, February 4, 2020, https://kb.isc.org/docs/aa-00924.

2. Wikipedia, "Dan Kaminsky," https://en.wikipedia.org/wiki/Dan_Kaminsky.

3. Nick Sullivan, "DNSSEC: An Introduction," *Cloudflare Blog*, October 7, 2014, https://blog.cloudflare.com/dnssec-an-introduction.

4. Almond and Conry, "CVE-2008-1447."

5. Sullivan, "DNSSEC: An Introduction."

6. Cloudflare, "DNS Security" (2021), www.cloudflare.com/learning/dns/dns-security.

Chapter 9: Controversy Around Encrypted DNS — DoT and DoH

1. Bennett and Tiwari, "Mozilla DNS over HTTPS (DoH) and Trusted Recursive Resolver (TRR)."

2. Victoria Risk, "Encrypted DNS: Why All the Drama About DoH?" Internet Systems Consortium, December 6, 2019, www.isc.org/blogs/doh-encrypted-dns.

3. Infoblox, "DoT and DoH Present New Challenges" (2019), www.infoblox.com/wp-content/uploads/infoblox-solution-note-dot-and-doh-present-new-challenges.pdf.

4. Sean Gallagher, "How to Keep Your ISP's Nose Out of Your Browser History with Encrypted DNS," *Ars Technica*, April 8, 2018, https://arstechnica.com/information-technology/2018/04/how-to-keep-your-isps-nose-out-of-your-browser-history-with-encrypted-dns.

5. Lee, "Why Big ISPs Aren't Happy About Google's Plans for Encrypted DNS."

6. Netmeister.org., "DNS Security: Threat Modeling DNSSEC, DoT, and DoH," October 10, 2019, www.netmeister.org/blog/doh-dot-dnssec.html.

7. Infoblox, "DoT and DoH Present New Challenges."

8. Risk, "Encrypted DNS: Why All the Drama About DoH?"

9. Darren Anstee, "Disappearing DNS: DoT and DoH, Where One Letter Makes a Great Difference," *Security*, February 6, 2020, www.securitymagazine.com/articles/91674-disappearing-dns-dot-and-doh-where-one-letter-makes-a-great-difference.

10. Bennett and Tiwari, "Mozilla DNS over HTTPS (DoH) and Trusted Recursive Resolver (TRR)."

11. Mike Schroll, "DoH Isn't Better, It's Just What Google Likes," DNSFilter, July 15, 2020, www.dnsfilter.com/blog/dns-over-tls.

12. Anstee, "Disappearing DNS."

13. Lily Hay Newman, "A Controversial Plan to Encrypt More of the Internet," *Wired*, October 9, 2019, www.wired.com/story/dns-over-https-encrypted-web.

14. Newman, "A Controversial Plan to Encrypt More of the Internet."

15. Gareth Corfield, "DoH! Mozilla Assures UK Minister that DNS-over-HTTPS Won't Be Default in Firefox for Britons," *The Register*, September 24, 2019, www.theregister.com/2019/09/24/mozilla_backtracks_doh_for_uk_users.

16. Catalin Cimpanu and Zero Day, "Apple Adds Support for Encrypted DNS (DoH and DoT)," *ZDNet*, June 25, 2020, www.zdnet.com/article/apple-adds-support-for-encrypted-dns-doh-and-dot.

Chapter 10: Solution — Diversify DNS Servers

1. Wikipedia, "Dan Kaminsky."

2. Joe Barr, "Patches Coming Today for DNS Vulnerability," Linux.com, July 8, 2008, https://web.archive.org/web/20090417004736/http://www.linux.com/feature/141080.

3. Risk, "Encrypted DNS: Why All the Drama About DoH?"

4. Jeftovic, "Turns Out Half the Internet Has a Single-Point-of-Failure Called 'Cloudflare.'"

5. Jelen, "The Top 5 Best DNS Servers for Improving Online Privacy & Security."

6. Performance, "Are More PoPs Better?" Section, November 2, 2016, www.section.io/blog/more-pops-cdns.

7. Performance, "Are More PoPs Better?"

8. Jeftovic, "DOS Attacks and DNS."

Chapter 11: The Argument for Control of Local DNS Servers by Government

1. David Lazarus, "The Pandemic Makes It Clear It's Time to Treat the Internet as a Utility," *Los Angeles Times*, October 23, 2020, www.latimes.com/business/story/2020-10-23/coronavirus-internet-is-a-utility.

2. Steve Andriole, "It's Time for an Internet-for-All Public Utility (Before Corona Crashes It," *Forbes*, March 30, 2020, www.forbes.com/sites/steveandriole/2020/03/30/its-time-for-an-internet-for-all-public-utility-before-corona-crashes-it/?sh=6e0786c0af95.

3. Craig MacKinder, "5 DNS Security Best Practices — What Every Growing Organization Needs to Know, May 2, 2020, https://craigmackinder.com/2020/05/02/5-dns-security-best-practices-what-every-growing-organization-needs-to-know.

4. Marybeth Miceli, "Obama Recalls Minneapolis Bridge Collapse, Media Blunders the Story," *Streetsblog USA*, April 21, 2011, https://usa.streetsblog.org/2011/04/21/obama-recalls-minneapolis-bridge-collapse-media-blunders-the-story.

5. Roberta Rampton, "Obama Pitches Plan to Fix Crumbling U.S. Roads, Bridges," *Reuters*, February 26, 2014, www.reuters.com/article/us-usa-transportation-obama/obama-pitches-plan-to-fix-crumbling-u-s-roads-bridges-idUSBREA1P0MO20140226.

6. "Crumbling Infrastructure: Examining the Challenges of Our Outdated and Overburdened Highways and Bridges: Hearing Before a Subcommittee of the Committee on Appropriations," United States Senate, One Hundred Thirteenth Congress First Session, Washington, D.C., June 13, 2013, www.govinfo.gov/content/pkg/CHRG-113shrg88752/html/CHRG-113shrg88752.htm.

7. Alicia M. Cohn, "Obama to Highlight 'Urgent' Bridge Repair in Boehner's Home State," *The Hill*, September 15, 2011, https://thehill.com/blogs/blog-briefing-room/news/181829-obama-to-highlight-urgent-bridge-repair-in-boehners-home-state.

8. Noam Maital, "U.S. Interstate Highway System: Why It Took 62 Years to Complete and How the Idea Arose in Germany," Waycare, September 5, 2018, https://waycaretech.com/us-interstate-highway-system-why-it-took-62-years-to-complete-and-how-the-idea-arose-in-germany.

9. Anne Stauffer and Kathryn de Wit, "Policymakers Should Consider Broadband Infrastructure a National Priority," *The Hill*, May 13, 2019, https://thehill.com/opinion/technology/443391-policymakers-should-consider-broadband-infrastructure-a-national-priority.

10. Maital, "U.S. Interstate Highway System."

11. Andriole, "It's Time for an Internet-for-All Public Utility (Before Corona Crashes It."

12. Tim Hornyak, "Crisis in America: A Crumbling Infrastructure," CNBC, November 21, 2013, www.cnbc.com/2013/11/21/crisis-in-america-a-crumbling-infrastructure.html.

13. Alyssa Davis, "In U.S., Most Oppose State Gas Tax Hike to Fund Repairs," Gallup, April 22, 2013, https://news.gallup.com/poll/161990/oppose-state-gas-tax-hike-fund-repairs.aspx.

14. Lazarus, "The Pandemic Makes It Clear It's Time to Treat the Internet as a Utility."

15. Jessica Walrack, "Need for Speed: Broadband for All Americans Is No Longer Optional," Wrkfrce, February 22, 2021, https://wrkfrce.com/the-need-for-speed-broadband-for-all-americans-is-no-longer-optional.

16. Lazarus, "The Pandemic Makes It Clear It's Time to Treat the Internet as a Utility."

17. Lazarus, "The Pandemic Makes It Clear It's Time to Treat the Internet as a Utility."

18. MacKinder, "5 DNS Security Best Practices."

19. Ephrat Livni, "The Coronavirus Crisis Proves the Internet Should Be a Public Utility," *Quartz*, March 26, 2020, https://qz.com/1826043/the-coronavirus-crisis-proves-internet-should-be-a-public-utility.

20. Lazarus, "The Pandemic Makes It Clear It's Time to Treat the Internet as a Utility."

21. Wikipedia, "Dan Kaminsky."

22. Lee, "Why Big ISPs Aren't Happy About Google's Plans for Encrypted DNS."

23. Lazarus, "The Pandemic Makes It Clear It's Time to Treat the Internet as a Utility."

24. Lazarus, "The Pandemic Makes It Clear It's Time to Treat the Internet as a Utility."

Chapter 12: The Role for Corporations

1. *SecurityWeek News*, "Everything You Need to Know About the SolarWinds Attack," January 8, 2021, www.securityweek.com/continuous-updates-everything-you-need-know-about-solarwinds-attack.

2. See Help Net Security, www.helpnetsecurity.com/2020/09/06/week-in-review-costliest-cybersecurity-failures-dns-hijacking-protection-aws-security-automation.

3. *SecurityWeek News*, "Everything You Need to Know About the SolarWinds Attack."

4. *SecurityWeek News*, "Everything You Need to Know About the SolarWinds Attack."

5. *SecurityWeek News*, "Everything You Need to Know About the SolarWinds Attack."

6. Risk, "Encrypted DNS: Why All the Drama About DoH?"

7. Risk, "Encrypted DNS: Why All the Drama About DoH?"

8. Timothy B. Lee, "DNS over HTTPS Will Make It Harder for ISPs to Monitor or Modify DNS Queries," *Ars Technica*, September 30, 2019, https://arstechnica.com/tech-policy/2019/09/isps-worry-a-new-chrome-feature-will-stop-them-from-spying-on-you.

9. Craig MacKinder, *Security and Privacy in an IT World: Managing and Meeting Online Regulatory Compliance in the 21st Century.* Toronto: Kinetics Design, 2017.

10. Newman, "A Controversial Plan to Encrypt More of the Internet."

11. Doug Drinkwater, "Does a Data Breach Really Affect Your Firm's Reputation?" *CSO*, January 7, 2016, www.csoonline.com/article/3019283/data-breach/does-a-data-breach-really-affect-your-firm-s-reputation.html.

12. Cybersecurity & Infrastructure Security Agency, "National Cyber Awareness System: Current Activity," March 8, 2017, www.us-cert.gov/ncas/current-activity.

13. Brian Krebs, "SolarWinds: What Hit Us Could Hit Others," *KrebsOnSecurity*, January 12, 2021, https://krebsonsecurity.com/2021/01/solarwinds-what-hit-us-could-hit-others.

14. Krebs, "SolarWinds: What Hit Us Could Hit Others."

15. MacKinder, "5 DNS Security Best Practices."

16. Lance Whitney, "How DNS Attacks Threaten Organizations," *TechRepublic*, June 10, 2020, www.techrepublic.com/article/how-dns-attacks-threaten-organizations.

17. Lazarus, "The Pandemic Makes It Clear It's Time to Treat the Internet as a Utility."

18. Lazarus, "The Pandemic Makes It Clear It's Time to Treat the Internet as a Utility."

19. Craig MacKinder, "The Case for Making Internet Service as a Public Utility in 2020," May 6, 2020, https://craigmackinder.com/2020/05/06/the-case-for-making-internet-service-as-a-public-utility-in-2020.

20. Michael J. Coren, "What Will Happen Now That Net Neutrality Is Gone? We Asked the Experts," *Quartz*, December 21, 2017, https://qz.com/1158328/what-will-happen-now-that-net-neutrality-is-gone-we-asked-the-experts.

21. Jeremy Singer-Vine and Kevin Collier, "Political Operatives Are Faking Voter Outrate with Millions of Made-Up Comments to Benefit the Rich and Powerful," *BuzzFeed News*, October 3, 2019, www.buzzfeednews.com/article/jsvine/net-neutrality-fcc-fake-comments-impersonation.

22. Jon Brodkin, "Comcast Does So Much Lobbying That It Says Disclosing It All Is Too Hard," *Ars Technica*, May 23, 2019, https://arstechnica.com/tech-policy/2019/05/comcast-does-so-much-lobbying-that-it-says-disclosing-it-all-is-too-hard.

23. David Elliot Berman and Victor Pickard, "Should the Internet Be a Public Utility? Hundreds of Cities Are Saying Yes," *Fast Company*, November 18, 2019, www.fastcompany.com/90432191/telecoms-wield- enormous-power-over-the-internet-but-cities-are-fighting-back.

Chapter 13: The Role for IT Security Professionals

1. (ISC)^2 is an international, nonprofit membership association for information security leaders. It's committed to helping its members learn, grow, and thrive. More than 150,000 certified members strong, it empowers professionals who touch every aspect of information security: https://www.isc2.org/About.

2. Vincent D'Angelo, "Why Today's Organizations Need a Domain Security Council," *Security*, October 19, 2020, www.securitymagazine.com/articles/93664-why-todays-organizations-need-a-domain-security-council.

3. Whitney, "How DNS Attacks Threaten Organizations."

4. Whitney, "How DNS Attacks Threaten Organizations."

5. D'Angelo, "Why Today's Organizations Need a Domain Security Council."

6. Infoblox, "DoT and DoH Present New Challenges."

7. Joseph Cox, "Comcast Is Lobbying Against Encryption That Could Prevent It from Learning Your Browsing History," *Vice*, October 23, 2109, www.vice.com/en_us/article/9kembz/comcast-lobbying-against-doh-dns-over-https-encryption-browsing-data.

8. Schroll, "DoH Isn't Better, It's Just What Google Likes."

9. Jon Brodkin, "Comcast, Mozilla Strike Privacy Deal to Encrypt DNS Lookups in Firefox," *Ars Technica*, June 25, 2020, https://arstechnica.com/tech-policy/2020/06/comcast-mozilla-strike-privacy-deal-to-encrypt-dns-lookups-in-firefox.

10. Brodkin, "Comcast, Mozilla Strike Privacy Deal to Encrypt DNS Lookups in Firefox."

11. Bennett and Tiwari, "Mozilla DNS over HTTPS (DoH) and Trusted Recursive Resolver (TRR)."

12. Neil J. Rubenking, "How (and Why) to Change Your DNS Server," *PCMag*, May 17, 2019, www.pcmag.com/how-to/how-and-why-to-change-your-dns-server.

13. Karl Bode, "Hoping to Combat ISP Snooping, Mozilla Enables Encrypted DNS," *Techdirt*, February 27, 2020, www.techdirt.com/articles/20200225/07382743978/hoping-to-combat-isp-snooping-mozilla-enables-encrypted-dns.shtml.

14. MacKinder, "5 DNS Security Best Practices."

15. D'Angelo, "Why Today's Organizations Need a Domain Security Council."

16. D'Angelo, "Why Today's Organizations Need a Domain Security Council."

17. Proofpoint Threat Insight Team, "PsiXBot Now Using Google DNS over HTTPS and Possible New Sexploitation Module," Proofpoint, September 6, 2019, www.proofpoint.com/us/threat-insight/post/psixbot-now-using-google-dns-over-https-and-possible-new-sexploitation-module.

18. Sergiu Gatlan, "New Godlua Malware Evades Traffic Monitoring via DNS over HTTPS," *BleepingComputer*, July 3, 2019, www.bleepingcomputer.com/news/security/new-godlua-malware-evades-traffic-monitoring-via-dns-over-https.

19. Patrick Howell O'Neill, "Trustico Revokes 23,000 SSL Certificates Due to Compromise," *CyberScoop*, February 28, 2018, www.cyberscoop.com/trustico-digicert-ssl-certificates-revoked.

20. Josephine Wolff, "How a 2011 Hack You've Never Heard of Changed the Internet's Infrastructure," *Slate*, December 21, 2016, https://slate.com/technology/2016/12/how-the-2011-hack-of-diginotar-changed-the-internets-infrastructure.html.

Chapter 14: Action Plan for DNS Public/Private Partnerships

1. Stephen Gandel, "Black and Poor Left Behind in Florida's Vaccine Rollout," *CBS News*, February 11, 2021, www.cbsnews.com/news/covid-vaccine-florida-wealthy-white-patients-poor-black.

2. Daria Litvinova, "'Telegram Revolution': App Helps Drive Belarus Protests," Associated Press, August 21, 2020, https://apnews.com/article/international-news-technology-business-ap-top-news-europe-823180da2b402f6a1dc9fbd76a6f476b.

3. Al Jazeera, "Timeline: How the Arab Spring Unfolded," January 14, 2021, www.aljazeera.com/news/2021/1/14/arab-spring-ten-years-on.

4. BBC News, "The Hong Kong Protests Explained in 100 and 500 Words," November 28, 2019, www.bbc.com/news/world-asia-china-49317695.

5. Emma Boyle, "UN Declares Online Freedom to Be a Human Right That Must be Protected," *Independent*, July 5, 2016, www.independent.co.uk/life-style/gadgets-and-tech/un-declares-online-freedom-to-be-a-human-right-that-must-be-protected-a7120186.html.

6. Associated Press, "'It's a Telegram Revolution': Messaging App Proves Crucial to Belarus," August 21, 2020, www.latimes.com/world-nation/story/2020-08-21/telegram-messaging-app-crucial-belarus-protests.

7. Livni, "The Coronavirus Crisis Proves the Internet Should Be a Public Utility."

8. KSBY News, "Kids Attend Classes in Car as Nipomo Family Struggles with At-Home Wi-Fi," August 20, 2020, https://youtu.be/Qib1oZSssrk.

9. Avi Asher-Schapiro, "'Our Education Lifeline': U.S. Battle over Broadband Heats Up," February 3, 2021, Reuters, www.reuters.com/article/us-tech-society-digital-divide-feature-t/our-education-lifeline-u-s-battle-over-broadband-heats-up-idUSKBN2A31RG.

10. Wikipedia, "Universal Service Fund," December 2, 2020, https://en.wikipedia.org/wiki/Universal_Service_Fund.

11. Wikipedia, "Universal Service Fund."

12. Wikipedia, "Universal Service Fund."

13. David Lazarus, "The Pandemic Makes Clear It's Time to Treat the Internet as a Utility," *Los Angeles Times*, October 23, 2020, www.latimes.com/business/story/2020-10-23/coronavirus-internet-is-a-utility.

14. Lifeline is the FCC's program to help make communications services more affordable for low-income consumers. Lifeline provides subscribers a discount on monthly telephone service, broadband Internet service, or bundled voice-broadband packages purchased from participating wireline or wireless providers. The discount helps ensure that low-income consumers can afford 21st-century broadband and the access it provides to jobs, health care, and educational resources: www.fcc.gov/lifeline-consumers.

15. Eduard Kovacs, "DNSpooq Flaws Expose Millions of Devices to DNS Cache Poisoning, Other Attacks," *SecurityWeek*, January 20, 2021, www.securityweek.com/dnspooq-flaws-expose-millions-devices-dns-cache-poisoning-other-attacks.

16. Associated Press, "Old Phone Booths Transformed into Wi-Fi Hotspots," January 1, 2016, www.cbsnews.com/news/phone-booths-transformed-into-wi-fi-hotspots.

17. Marvin G. Perez, Michael Hirtzer, and Deena Shanker, "Smashing Eggs, Dumping Milk: Farmers Waste More Food Than Ever," *Bloomberg Green*, May 18, 2020, www.bloomberg.com/news/articles/2020-05-18/smashing-eggs-dumping-milk-farmers-waste-more-food-than-ever.

18. Tom Fogden, "Why Chattanooga Has the Fastest Internet in the US," Tech.co, August 21, 2018, https://tech.co/news/chattanooga-fastest-internet-usa-2018-08.

19. Stauffer and de Wit, "Policymakers Should Consider Broadband Infrastructure a National Priority."

20. Stauffer and de Wit, "Policymakers Should Consider Broadband Infrastructure a National Priority."

21. Andriole, "It's Time for an Internet-for-All Public Utility (Before Corona Crashes It)."

22. Jon Brodkin, "Democrats Try to Ban Internet Shutoffs Until Pandemic Is Over," *Ars Technica*, May 12, 2020, https://arstechnica.com/tech-policy/2020/05/democrats-try-to-ban-internet-shutoffs-until-pandemic-is-over.

23. Andriole, "It's Time for an Internet-for-All Public Utility (Before Corona Crashes It)."

24. Brianna Chavez, "El Paso's Not Seeing Power Outages Like the Rest of Texas — Here's Why," KVIA.com, February 15, 2021, https://kvia.com/news/el-paso/2021/02/15/el-pasos-not-seeing-power-outages-like-the-rest-of-texas-and-heres-why.

Essential Terms We Need to Know — DNS Cheat Sheet

1. The Domain Name Registration Data Lookup conducts Registration Data Access Protocol (RDAP) queries. RDAP enables users to access current registration data and was created as an eventual replacement for the WHOIS protocol. The results displayed come directly from registry operators and/or registrars in real time. ICANN doesn't generate, collect, retain, or store any data associated with an RDAP compliant lookup. If the queried information isn't available in RDAP, the query will be redirected to whois.icann.org (WHOIS failover lookup). In cases of WHOIS failover lookups, ICANN may generate, collect, retain, or store the domain name queried and the results for the transitory duration necessary to show results in response to real-time queries: https://lookup.icann.org.

Glossary

AP: Associated Press
APNIC: Asia Pacific Network Information Centre
ARPANET: Advanced Research Projects Agency Network
ASCE: American Society of Civil Engineers

BIND: Berkeley Internet Name Domain

CCTV: Closed-Circuit Television
CISA: Cybersecurity and Infrastructure Security Agency (United States)
CISO: Chief Information Security Officer
CPE: Customer Premise Equipment

DARPA: Defense Advanced Research Projects Agency
DDoS: Distributed Denial of Service
DHS: Department of Homeland Security
DNS: Domain Name System
DNSSEC: Domain Name System Security Extensions
DoH: Domain Name System over Hypertext Transfer Protocol
DoT: Domain Name System over Transport Layer Security
DVR: Digital Video Recording

EFF: Electronic Frontier Foundation
EPP: Extensible Provisioning Protocol

FBI: Federal Bureau of Investigation
FCC: Federal Communications Commission

GDPR: General Data Protection Regulation

HIPPA: Heath Insurance Portability and Accountability Act
HTTP: Hypertext Transfer Protocol
HTTPS: Hypertext Transfer Protocol Secure

IAB: Internet Architecture Board
IANA: Internet Assigned Numbers Authority
ICANN: Internet Corporation for Assigned Names and Numbers
IDC: International Data Corporation
IETF: Internet Engineering Task Force
IGF: Internet Governance Forum
IP: Internet Protocol
ISC: Internet Systems Consortium
ISP: Internet Service Provider
IT: Information Technology

LACNIC: Latin America and Caribbean Network Information Centre

MAD: Mutually Assured Destruction
Mbps: Megabits per Second
MNO: Mobile Network Operator
MX: Mail Exchanger

NTIA: National Telecommunications and Information Administration

PCH: Packet Clearing House
PN: Proactive Nameserver
PoP: Point of Presence
POP: Post Office Protocol
POS: Point of Sale
PPE: Personal Protection Equipment

RDAP: Registration Data Access Protocol
RFC: Request for Comment
RIPE: Réseaux IP Européens
RIR: Regional Internet Registry
RO: Registry Operator
RR: Resource Record

SIEM: Security Information and Event Management
SLD: Second Level Domain
SPKI: Simple Public Key Infrastructure
SRI: Stanford Research Institute
SRI-NIC: Stanford Research Institute — Network Information Center
SSL: Secure Sockets Layer
SSRF: Server-Side Request Forgery

TCP: Transmission Control Protocol
TLD: Top Level Domain
TLS: Transport Layer Security
TRR: Trusted Recursive Resolver
TTL: Time to Live

UCLA: University of California at Los Angeles
UDP: User Datagram Protocol
UIAF: "Universal Internet Access Fund"
URL: Uniform Resource Locator
US-CERT: United States Computer Emergency Readiness Team
USDA: U.S. Department of Agriculture
USF: Universal Service Fund

VPN: Virtual Private Network
VR: Virtual Reality

Wi-Fi: Wireless Fidelity
WS: Websocket
WSIS: World Summit on the Information Society
WWW: World Wide Web

Acknowledgments

I would first like to thank my children and my loving wife for supporting me through my many endeavors, including this book. They have accommodated my dynamic IT career for many years. That has meant that I might need to drop everything and investigate a cybersecurity incident or remediate a new IT problem without much notice. Despite some unexpected scheduling changes, they continue to be supportive and encouraging, and always accommodating to my schedule. Without their accommodations, encouragement, and support, this book wouldn't have been completed.

As with my first book, *Security and Privacy in an IT World*, I wish to express my gratitude and appreciation to all the writing consultants whose work has contributed to the writing and inspiration for this book, as well as to the researchers, editor, and designer. I started, stopped, revised, returned, and started again several times on this second book. At each milestone, these colleagues encouraged my triumph over each challenge until I once again resumed the laborious task of telling this story about Domain Name System security.

Malika Dickerson labored intensely through surveys, legislation, and publications to find the facts included herein. Her scholarly viewpoints and intellect contributed much to the development of my opinions regarding the politics of regulatory compliance legislation.

Michael Carroll provided his editing services for this book. His perseverance and dedication to his craft are truly remarkable. I am grateful for his professionalism and dedication throughout the process.

I want to extend an extremely large thank-you to Daniel Crack. His vast experience in graphic design and typesetting literally made this book into a much more enjoyable experience. I'm fortunate to have such a talented book designer to make this book both beautiful and readable. Daniel's production services are simply amazing.

I would also like to thank my clients, employers, and colleagues who have bestowed upon me the responsibility of cybersecurity and IT governance. I'm grateful for your support while we figured out how to most effectively take care of the needs of the business while meeting our compliance and security requirements.

Index